Table of Contents

Introduction

What Is Readers' Theater?

One good way to gain an understanding of readers' theater is to first get a clear picture of what it is *not*. Readers' theater is not a fully-staged production with sets, costumes, and dramatic action performed by actors who memorize lines from a script. Instead, a readers' theater performance is a dramatic reading, just as its name suggests. Readers are usually seated, reading from a script that is held in their hands or placed on a music stand in front of them. There may be minimal use of costumes or props, such as hats, a scepter or crown, or a simple backdrop to provide a suggestion of the setting and characters that the readers hope to bring to life for the audience during their dramatic reading.

Readers' theater offers all the enrichment of traditional theater productions, but without the logistical challenges that come with designing and building sets and creating costumes. Students are spared the stress of having to memorize lines, and can instead focus on developing a strong dramatic reading of the script.

How to Integrate *Readers' Theater* into Your Classroom

The *Readers' Theater* scripts may be used in a variety of settings for a range of educational purposes. Consider the following:

Language Arts blocks are ideal for incorporating *Readers' Theater* scripts, with their emphasis on reading aloud with expression. Many of the follow-up activities that accompany each script address key skills from the reading/language arts curriculum.

Content-Area Instruction can come alive when you use a *Readers' Theater* script to help explore social studies, science, or math concepts. Check the Table of Contents for the grade-level content-area connections in each script.

Integrated Thematic Teaching can continue throughout the day when you use *Readers' Theater* scripts to help you maintain your thematic focus across all areas of the curriculum, from language arts instruction through content-area lessons.

School Assemblies and Holiday Programs provide the perfect opportunity to showcase student performances. Consider presenting a *Readers' Theater* performance for Black History Month, Women's History Month, for parent evenings, or any other occasion when your students are invited to perform.

Teaching the *Readers' Theater* Units

The 15 units in this volume each include the following:

• A **teacher page** to help you plan instruction:

A short **summary** gives you an overview of each script's plot.

Use the **number of parts** to choose the number of readers to assign per role. Or, you may wish to create two or more casts for each production.

Background information provides facts that you may need to know about the subject treated in the script. It also guides you in activating students' prior knowledge or in building background about new or unfamiliar topics. This helps promote success for students as they approach each new script.

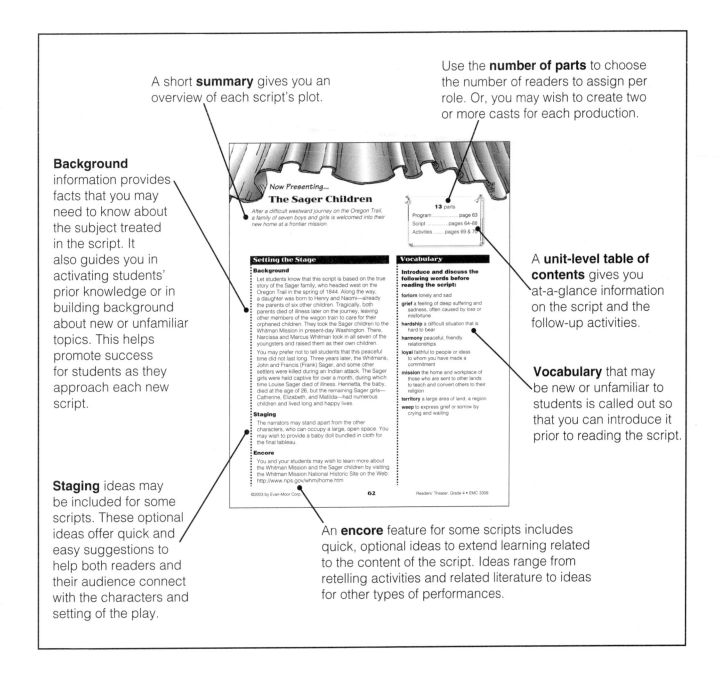

A **unit-level table of contents** gives you at-a-glance information on the script and the follow-up activities.

Vocabulary that may be new or unfamiliar to students is called out so that you can introduce it prior to reading the script.

Staging ideas may be included for some scripts. These optional ideas offer quick and easy suggestions to help both readers and their audience connect with the characters and setting of the play.

An **encore** feature for some scripts includes quick, optional ideas to extend learning related to the content of the script. Ideas range from retelling activities and related literature to ideas for other types of performances.

- A reproducible **program** page provides an introduction to the script and a list of characters. Use this page to list the names of students who will read each role, and distribute it to your audience to enhance the theater-going experience.

- The **script** is the heart of the *Readers' Theater* volume. This is the reproducible four- or five-page text that students will read during rehearsals and performances. You may wish to read the script aloud to students before assigning parts and beginning rehearsal readings. Once you have read through the script as a group, you may wish to assign students to work independently in small groups while you interact with other student groups.

- Two or three pages of follow-up **activities** may be assigned once students have completed a first reading of the script. Activities are designed to be completed independently, and may be conducted while you provide individualized or small-group instruction or hold a rehearsal with another group of students.

Meeting Individual Needs

Struggling readers may be partnered with one or more stronger readers who all read the same role together. This group support is often enough to allow struggling readers to participate fully in the activity. Struggling readers may also be able to independently read parts that have a repeating refrain or a simple rhyme pattern.

Students acquiring English may benefit from using the same approaches as for struggling readers. In addition, you may wish to create an audio recording of the script to provide English learners the opportunity to listen to fluent English pronunciation of the script as they follow along with the written text.

Accelerated learners may be challenged to transform *Readers' Theater* scripts into fully-staged productions by adding stage directions, planning props and sets, and even developing or expanding the existing dialog. You might also use such students as "directors," helping to manage small-group rehearsals for class *Readers' Theater* productions.

Evaluating Student Performance

Use the templates provided on pages 5 and 6 to help students plan and evaluate their performances. You may copy and distribute the templates just as they are, or use them to guide you in leading a class discussion about the criteria for evaluating *Readers' Theater* performances. Students may also develop their own iconography (e.g., one or two thumbs up, thumbs down, 1 to 5 stars, etc.) to rate their own performances and those of their classmates. Encourage students to be thoughtful in providing feedback, stressing the importance of sharing ways to improve, as well as highlighting successful aspects of the performance. You may wish to conduct performance reviews during the rehearsal stage in order to give students an opportunity to incorporate suggestions for improvement. You may also wish to compare those comments to feedback following the final performance. Use the template on page 7 to conduct your own assessment of students' acquisition of language arts skills during *Readers' Theater* activities.

NOTE: Reproduce this page so each student can check off the various steps in preparing a *Readers' Theater* performance.

Pre-performance Checklist

Name _____

1. Did you listen to or participate in a first reading of the script?
   ☐ **Yes**
   ☐ **No** – Watch a group rehearsal if hearing the script aloud is helpful for you.

2. Did you highlight all your lines in the script?
   ☐ **Yes**
   ☐ **No** – Use a highlighting pen to go over all your lines.

3. Did you mark places where you must pause between lines?
   ☐ **Yes**
   ☐ **No** – Use a mark like this: / /

4. Have you collected any materials or props that you will use?
   ☐ **Yes**
   ☐ **No** – Ask your teacher or other cast members for ideas if you need help.

5. Have you chosen and practiced any movements, faces, or speaking styles you will use?
   ☐ **Yes**
   ☐ **No** – Ask your teacher or other cast members for ideas if you need help.

6. Have you practiced reading your lines with expression?
   ☐ **Yes**
   ☐ **No** – Try out your ideas with a partner or another cast member.

7. Have you participated in a rehearsal and gotten performance feedback?
   ☐ **Yes**
   ☐ **No** – Have a reviewer focus on your participation in the play. After you get feedback, find ways to make changes to improve your performance.

Performance Review Template

Date: _____   Title of play: _____

☐ Rehearsal
☐ Performance
1. I am reviewing
    ☐ one reader   Name: _____ Role: _____
    ☐ the entire performance

2. I could see the reader(s).
    ☐ Yes
    ☐ Needs improvement   Name(s): _____

3. I could hear the reader(s).
    ☐ Yes
    ☐ Needs to speak more loudly   Name(s): _____

4. I could understand the reader(s).
    ☐ Yes
    ☐ Needs to speak more clearly   Name(s): _____

5. The reader(s) used good expression.
    ☐ Yes
    ☐ Needs to improve   Name(s): _____

6. The use of gestures was
    ☐ just right
    ☐ not enough; use more
    ☐ too much; use fewer   Name(s): _____

7. Some things that were done well:

_____

_____

8. Some things that could be done better, and some ideas for improving them:

_____

_____

NOTE: Reproduce this teacher page to assess student acquisition of the following *Readers' Theater* skills.

Assessing Oral Presentations

As you observe students during rehearsals or performances, focus on the following areas in assessing individual students.

Date: _____

Title of play: _____

☐ Rehearsal

☐ Performance

Name: _____   Role: _____

1. Student speaks clearly.   ☐ Yes   ☐ Needs improvement

2. Student speaks at appropriate pace.   ☐ Yes   ☐ Needs improvement

3. Student speaks fluently, using appropriate
   intonation, expression, and emphasis.   ☐ Yes   ☐ Needs improvement

4. Student enlivens reading with gestures
   and facial expressions.   ☐ Yes   ☐ Needs improvement

5. Student prepared and used
   appropriate props.   ☐ Yes   ☐ Not applicable

6. Student participated actively in
   rehearsals.   ☐ Yes   ☐ Needs improvement

7. Student contributed appropriately
   to this production.   ☐ Yes   ☐ Needs improvement

Other comments: _____

_____

_____

_____

Now Presenting...

Louis Pasteur:
A Scientist Serving Humanity

As a child, Louis Pasteur longed to unlock the secrets of diseases that made people suffer. He studied hard and became a gifted scientist who made enormous contributions to the world of science and medicine. Over 100 years later, his discoveries continue to save lives all around the world.

Setting the Stage

Background

Invite students to share what they know about vaccines and vaccination. Be sure they understand that the natural defenses of the body's immune system create antibodies when they come in contact with germs. Vaccination introduces weakened forms of certain germs into the body. The body fights these germs and develops immunity to them. Vaccination has saved millions of people from experiencing the terrible diseases that meant almost certain death prior to the development of vaccines.

Staging

Provide simple props for the person reading the part of Louis. The young Louis could hold a ball or toy truck. The adult Louis could wear a lab coat. You might have the actors taking the role of doctors wear stethoscopes around their necks.

Vocabulary

Introduce and discuss the following words before reading the script:

germ: a microscopic organism, such as bacteria, that can cause disease

laboratory: a room or building used for scientific experimentation or research

mad: having rabies

prominent: well known and respected

rabies: a severe infectious disease that attacks the central nervous system of mammals and can be transmitted to people through the bite of an infected animal

vaccination: the administration or application of a vaccine

vaccine: a preparation of weakened organisms that is introduced into the body to produce immunity to a specific disease by causing the body to form antibodies

Now Presenting...

Louis Pasteur:
A Scientist Serving Humanity

A devoted scientist struggles to rid the world of terrible diseases. His amazing discoveries still affect our lives today.

Characters

Narrator 1 .... _____

Narrator 2 .... _____

Louis .... _____

Mama .... _____

Papa... _____

Marie (Louis's wife) .... _____

Mrs. Meister .... _____

Joseph Meister .... _____
(a nine-year-old boy)

Doctor 1 .... _____

Doctor 2 .... _____

Louis Pasteur:
A Scientist Serving Humanity

.... **Characters** ....

Narrator 1   Marie

Narrator 2   Mrs. Meister

Louis   Joseph Meister

Mama   Doctor 1

Papa   Doctor 2

Narrator 1: Louis Pasteur was a French scientist who was born in 1822. During his lifetime he worked tirelessly to learn about germs. He learned that certain germs caused diseases.

Narrator 2: Louis Pasteur learned that he could grow germs in his laboratory. He could find a way to weaken the germs. Then he could inject the weakened germs into a healthy animal.

Narrator 1: The animal could fight off the weakened germs and not get sick. This process was called *vaccination*.

Narrator 2: Louis Pasteur did not invent vaccination. But he was the first to discover how to make vaccines from germs. His work has saved millions of lives all over the world.

Narrator 1: Even after solving the riddle of many diseases, Louis was still not satisfied. Toward the end of his life, he was determined to conquer one more disease: the deadly disease of rabies. His interest in this awful disease began when he was a small boy in a French village.

Mama: Louis, quick come in the house!

Louis: Why, Mama? I am playing.

Papa: *(somewhat angrily)* Now, Louis. Hurry. Don't argue!

Narrator 2: Hearing Papa's angry tone, Louis quickly obeyed. As he reached the doorway, his father pulled the boy inside and slammed the door. His mother hugged him and smiled at him, but he could see the worry in her eyes.

Louis: What's wrong, Papa? What's happening?

Papa: Come with me.

Narrator 1: Papa and Mama led Louis to the upper floor of the old house. From the window they could see most of the village. On the next street, Louis saw a fearsome sight.

Louis: It's a wolf, Papa! What is a wolf doing in the village? Wolves run in the woods, not here in our village.

Papa: That is no ordinary wolf, Louis. Look at him and tell me what you see.

Louis: He's very thin, isn't he, Papa? And look! Why does he have white foam around his mouth?

Papa: The wolf is sick. He has rabies. Anyone he bites will surely die.

Narrator 1: As Louis and his parents watched in horror, a woman from the village turned the corner into the street. The rabid wolf turned on her at once, biting her on the hand. Screaming, the woman broke free and ran into the nearest shop.

Mama: Oh, this is terrible. Come away now, Louis. This is not a sight for your young eyes.

Narrator 2: Mama drew Louis away from the window, but the scene haunted him for the rest of his life.

Narrator 1: Louis grew up and went to school. He was an average student during his early years. He showed great talent as an artist, and even considered a career as a portrait artist. However, as he began his advanced studies, he developed a deep interest in the world of science.

Narrator 2: His work on germs and their role in causing disease soon earned him great respect and fame throughout France and Europe. Louis and his wife settled in Paris, where he taught and continued his research. In time, he found answers to terrible diseases such as cholera and anthrax.

Narrator 2: Finally, in 1882, Louis was ready to turn his full attention to conquering rabies, the dreaded disease that had haunted him since childhood. He and his assistants developed shots that would prevent rabies in animals. Even if an animal had already been bitten, a series of Pasteur's special shots could stop the disease. One big question remained, however. Louis talked it over with his wife.

Louis: Will my shots work to stop rabies in people? I wonder . . .

Marie: Have patience, Louis.

Louis: I don't have time for patience, Marie! I am growing old and tired. I am over 60 years old already, and I want to finish this work!

Marie: I know, Louis. Your work is very important. But it is time for you to rest and let others carry on the work.

Louis: I can't put the responsibility on others. Perhaps . . . perhaps I will test the rabies shots on myself.

Marie: Louis, you can't be serious. What a dreadful idea! I could not bear such a thing!

Louis: I'm sorry, Marie. I know it's a crazy idea and I don't mean to upset you. It's just that I see time slipping away. I must find the answer.

Marie: It will come, Louis. Have patience.

Louis: *(sighing)* I will try.

Narrator 1: A few days later, Louis is working alone in his laboratory. Suddenly, there is a knock at the door.

Louis: Come in. May I help you?

Mrs. Meister: Dr. Pasteur, I am Mrs. Meister and this is my son, Joseph. We have come a long way to see you. I have read about your work with rabies. We need your help.

Louis: Sit down, please. Joseph, tell me what happened.

Joseph: *(fearfully)* A mad dog bit me, sir. It was horrible. His lips were all foamy and his eyes were wild. Am I going to get sick? Will I die?

Mrs. Meister: *(tearfully)* Please, Dr. Pasteur, please help my son.

Louis: *(kindly)* This is a very difficult situation. You see, we can't be sure that your son has caught the disease.

Mrs. Meister: If we wait for him to become ill, it will be too late. He was severely bitten. The dog was definitely mad. We can't take a chance!

Louis: Mrs. Meister, you must understand. The shots themselves might make Joseph sick. They have never been tried on a person.

Mrs. Meister: But they are our only hope. I am convinced of it.

Louis: I am going to ask some doctors here in Paris to come and see Joseph. Let us see what they have to say about the matter.

Narrator 2: Louis sends for two prominent doctors. They hurry to the laboratory and examine Joseph.

Doctor 1: Indeed, Pasteur, I believe that this boy will die unless you help him.

Doctor 2: Yes, I agree. The shots may not help him, but they cannot hurt him.

Doctor 1: We have no medicines that can help. You must try.

Doctor 2: Good luck to all of you.

Mrs. Meister: Will you do it? Will you give Joseph the shots?

Louis: Yes. Yes, of course. There is nothing else to be done.

Joseph: Thank you, sir. Thank you. I am sure the shots will work!

Narrator 1: Louis patted the boy's shoulder and smiled at him, but his heart was filled with fear.

Narrator 2: Louis gave Joseph a series of shots. Each one was stronger than the last. After each shot, Pasteur would worry and fret. His fear was so great that he could hardly sleep at night. Would Joseph get sick? Would the vaccine fail? Weeks went by, and Joseph remained healthy.

Louis: The shots are finished, Joseph. You were very brave. I am going to let you go home now, but you must promise to write to me every other day. Let me know how you are feeling.

Mrs. Meister: We are deeply grateful, Dr. Pasteur. There is no way to repay you for what you have done.

Joseph: Thank you, sir. Thank you for saving my life!

Louis: I hope we have been successful, but I am not quite sure. Take care of yourself, Joseph, and don't forget to write!

Narrator 1: Weeks passed, and then months, and still the letters came. Joseph was healthy. The shots had worked! Louis reported his results to the Academy of Sciences. Newspapers printed the story. People from all over the world began coming to Paris for treatment. Louis tried to help them all.

Marie: Louis, you are working too hard. You cannot possibly care for all these people.

Louis: You are right, my dear. I have asked the Academy of Sciences to build a special laboratory. They have agreed. With more money and more scientists and doctors, more people will get help. And I can retire.

Marie: Yes, Louis. It is time. You have done enough. Your work will help thousands of people to live healthier lives. I am so proud of you!

Name _____

Thank You, Thank You

It is easy to understand why Joseph Meister was very grateful to Louis Pasteur. After all, Louis Pasteur saved Joseph's life. But Louis Pasteur was probably grateful to Joseph too. Why do you think this might be so?

Imagine that you are Joseph, and write a thank-you note to Louis Pasteur.

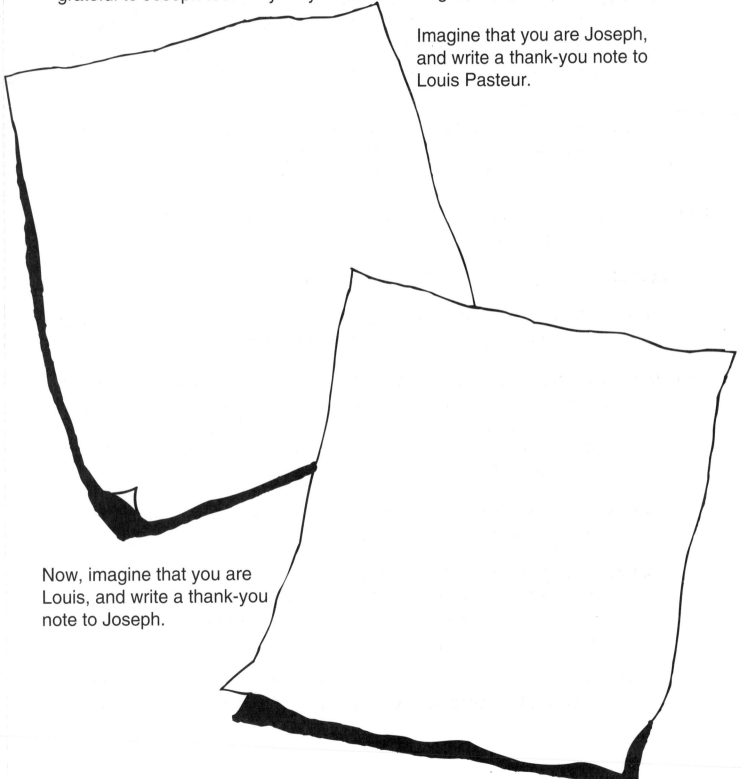

Now, imagine that you are Louis, and write a thank-you note to Joseph.

15

Pasteur's Process

Louis Pasteur discovered that microbes in milk can make people sick. He also discovered that these microbes can be destroyed by heating the milk. Unscramble these words, and then use the circled letters in order to spell the name of the process Pasteur discovered for making milk safer.

reustap ⃝ _ _ _ _ _ _ _

charseer _ _ _ _ ⃝ _ _ _ _

smerg _ _ _ ⃝ _

thoss _ _ _ ⃝ _

nafcer _ _ _ _ ⃝ _

silou _ _ ⃝ _ _

trabicea _ _ _ _ ⃝ _ _ _

seencic _ _ ⃝ _ _ _ _

uzenimmi _ _ _ _ _ _ ⃝ _ _

sadisee _ _ _ _ ⃝ _ _

toybroalar _ _ _ _ _ _ ⃝ _ _ _ _

sabier _ _ _ ⃝ _ _

crombie _ _ _ _ ⃝ _ _

cancive _ _ _ _ _ _ ⃝ _

Word Box

shots
disease
bacteria
microbe
Pasteur
rabies
France
science
research
Louis
germs
vaccine
laboratory
immunize

The process was called

_ _ _ _ _ _ _ _ _ _ _ _ _ _

Now Presenting...

The Girls of the Round Table

A group of fourth-grade girls organize a service club after learning about the Knights of the Round Table and their commitment to doing good.

Setting the Stage

Background

Invite students to share what they know about King Arthur and the Knights of the Round Table. You may need to tell them that historians still debate whether Arthur was a real king or merely a mythic figure. Discuss the importance of the stories that developed around Arthur, Camelot, and the Knights of the Round Table—stories in which virtue is rewarded, evil is thwarted, and right matters more than might.

Staging

For the media center scene, seat readers at a round table or at desks arranged in a circle. If possible, provide a book with illustrations of Camelot, knights, and medieval art. For the playground scene, have one of the boys hold a football.

Vocabulary

Introduce and discuss the following words before reading the script:

Camelot: the English town in which King Arthur's court was located

chivalry: a demonstration of noble qualities, such as courage, honor, and loyalty

emblem: a visual symbol that represents an idea

Excalibur: the name of King Arthur's sword

joust: a combat between two knights with lances while on horseback

knight: in the Middle Ages, a nobleman who provided military service to his king

medieval: from the Middle Ages

Now Presenting...

The Girls of the Round Table

Inspired by the Knights of the Round Table, a group of elementary-school girls form a club to perform good deeds.

Characters

Narrator .... _____

Kristin .... _____

Jennifer .... _____

Maria .... _____

Burthia...................................... _____

Lin .... _____

Mr. Hall..................................... _____
(Media Center Specialist)

Art .... _____
(a boy on the playground)

Ramon .... _____
(a boy on the playground)

Lamont .... _____
(a boy on the playground)

Readers' Theater, Grade 4 • EMC 3309

The Girls of the Round Table

·························· **Characters** ··························

Narrator	Lin
Kristin	Mr. Hall
Jennifer	Art
Maria	Ramon
Burthia	Lamont

Narrator: Five fourth-grade girls sit in a circle in the school Media Center. They are looking at pictures of castles in a book about Camelot.

Kristin: Wouldn't it be wonderful to live in a castle?

Jennifer: Oh, yes! I'd love to be a princess and wear those beautiful dresses. And I'd *really* love to meet a real-life prince!

Maria: *(sighing)* And wouldn't it be wonderful to have a knight perform noble and heroic deeds for you?

Burthia: Are you kidding? I'd like to perform noble and heroic deeds myself! What kinds of things did knights do?

Maria: They rode horses and jousted! Knights pledged to be loyal to the king, to stand up against evil, and to perform acts of chivalry.

Lin: Chivalry? What's that?

Jennifer: Chivalry was the code that knights lived by. It was like an oath. The knights promised to be good and honorable, and they promised to always help people in need.

Lin: Oh! You mean like the Knights of the Round Table?

Narrator: Lin takes the book and flips to another page.

Lin: *(pointing to a picture in the book)* See? These are the legendary Knights of the Round Table. They performed virtuous deeds, like defending the helpless and protecting the kingdom from invaders.

Maria: My little brother heard those stories at school. Now all he wants to do is slay dragons and rescue damsels in distress. My dad even made him a little shield with an emblem on it.

Burthia: My little brother must have heard the same stories. I'm starting to run out of noble things he can do at home to show his chivalry!

Maria: King Arthur's knights performed acts of chivalry too. Each knight wore an emblem of a dragon and a round table.

Kristin: I wonder what the round table was all about. It seems like it was really important to them.

Lin: *(pointing to the book)* The emblem was the symbol of the Knights of the Round Table. The table was special because a round table makes everybody equal. Nobody sits at the head of the table, not even the king.

Kristin: Hey! We're sitting at a round table. Burthia's right. We *could* be like the knights in the book! We could all promise to do good deeds.

Maria: *(chuckling)* You mean like helping old people cross the street?

Kristin: Well, sure . . . helping elders is certainly kind and honorable. But I was thinking more about helping people here at school. My cousin Lisa is in sixth grade over at the middle school, and she's a Peacemaker. She helps people work out their disagreements and avoid getting into fights. I guess she's kind of like a knight.

Burthia: Let's do it! Let's start a club for chivalry! We can call ourselves the Girls of the Round Table!

Lin: The Girls of the Round Table! What a great idea!

Narrator: The girls laugh and talk excitedly about their new club. Mr. Hall, the Media Center Specialist, walks over to their table.

Mr. Hall: Girls! Have you forgotten that you're in the Media Center? What are you talking about so loudly?

Burthia: We're the Girls of the Round Table! We're going to be like the knights in this book and perform heroic acts and help people.

Maria: *(taking the book)* But in these pictures all the knights are wearing armor, and King Arthur even has an enchanted sword called Excalibur. We don't have any of that stuff!

Mr. Hall: *(kindly)* You don't need armor to be chivalrous. You just have to do the right thing—even if it's hard. A commitment to helping people is every bit as important today as it was in medieval times.

Kristin: But who are *we* going to help? The knights in this book stood up against evil!

Mr. Hall: Why don't you go outside and enjoy the last 10 minutes of recess? Maybe you'll find someone who needs your help.

Narrator: The girls leave the Media Center and head to the playground.

Lin: Do you think we'll find someone who needs our help? Is there really a place for chivalry here at school?

Burthia: I'm sure there must be *somebody* who could use a knight!

Narrator: Just then the girls notice a group of children gathering around three boys who are arguing loudly. One of them holds a football. Another moves toward the ball, ready to snatch it away.

Burthia: Hold it, guys! Let's not get physical! What's this all about?

Art: *(holding the ball)* What do you care? Back off! I'm not about to let this wimp steal my turn!

Ramon: Who are you calling a wimp, loser? I said I was going to be quarterback after Lamont, so get over it already.

Art: I don't think so, whiner. And in case you haven't noticed, I'm the one with the ball. *(taunting)* Or do you think you can take it from me?

Narrator: As Ramon lunges at Art, Burthia and Lin step between them.

Lin: Hey, guys, there's got to be a better way to work this out. We can't have all the younger kids see you fifth-graders fighting like toddlers!

Kristin: You know that our school has a zero-tolerance policy for physical aggression.

Lamont: What's it to you, anyway? We don't need any little kids like you telling us how to act.

Maria: Well, if you know so much, why can't you figure out a way to work out your problem without shoving and calling names?

Ramon: What do you care? Why don't you mind your own business!

Burthia: Keeping the peace and helping people settle their differences *is* our business.

Lamont: What are you talking about?

Jennifer: We're the Girls of the Round Table, and it's our business to see that people at this school work out their problems peacefully. Now, do you think the three of you can figure out a way to do that, or would you like us to offer you some suggestions?

Art: Girls of the Round Table? What's up with that?

Lin: It's not really that complicated. We help people settle disagreements and find ways to avoid getting into fights.

Ramon: Oh yeah? Well what fair solution do you have for this situation?

Kristin: Well, how about this: since there are only five minutes of recess left, and since Lamont already had a turn as quarterback, why don't you and Art each take two minutes to play quarterback?

Art: Hey, kid—that sounds fine to me. Since I've got the ball, I'll just go first so we don't waste any *more* time.

Ramon: I guess I can go for that.

Lamont: Well, let's get going before we run out of time!

Narrator: As the three boys return to their game, the Girls of the Round Table look at each other in disbelief.

Burthia: That was awesome! We actually prevented a fight!

Jennifer: *(to Kristin)* You did some quick thinking to come up with that!

Kristin: There's always a way to work things out.

Lin: *(ironically)* I noticed that they didn't bother to thank us for our help.

Maria: Well, knights don't expect anything in return for their good deeds. Their reward is knowing that they've done the right thing.

Burthia: You know what? It really does feel good, doesn't it?

Jennifer, Kristin, Lin, and Maria: Yes! It sure does!

Narrator: The bell rings, signaling the end of recess. As the Girls of the Round Table walk toward their class, the football players run past them.

Ramon: Hey, kid—you know something? You're OK!

Art: Yeah, thanks for keeping me in line back there. Getting into a fight with Ramon would *not* have been cool!

Narrator: As the boys disappear around a corner, the Girls of the Round Table look at each other, awestruck.

Burthia: Can you believe that?

Lin: You know what? I think chivalry just might turn out to be contagious!

Jennifer: Long live the Girls of the Round Table!

Lin, Burthia, Maria, and Kristin: Long live the Girls of the Round Table!

Name _____

Emblems of Chivalry

The Knights of the Round Table had an emblem that symbolized chivalry. King Arthur gave his knights the emblem to help them remember to do the right thing.

- The cross represents purity and goodness.
- The red dragon stands for King Arthur, whose last name was Pendragon.
- The Round Table symbolizes the equality and unity of the knights.

Draw an emblem for the Girls of the Round Table to help them remember to do the right thing. Be sure your emblem includes at least three symbols. Use the writing lines to describe what each of your symbols represent.

Name _____

Good Deeds

You don't have to be a medieval knight to be chivalrous. Each time you do something good for someone else, you are performing an act of chivalry.

Use this chart to help you think about good deeds you've done for others, good deeds that others have done for you, and good deeds that you'd like to do in the future. Write 5 to 10 good deeds in each column. Remember, good deeds can help people, animals, or our planet.

Good Deeds I Have Done for Others	Good Deeds Others Have Done for Me	Good Deeds I Will Do in the Future

Now Presenting...

The Farmer, His Son, and Their Donkey

A farmer and his son learn an important lesson: If you try to please everybody, you will end up pleasing nobody—especially yourself!

Setting the Stage

Background

Make sure students understand that fables are short stories that contain a message or lesson. The message is sometimes called the "moral" of the story. The characters in fables are people or animals whose experiences illustrate this moral.

Tell students that many fables are believed to have been written by Aesop, a slave who lived in ancient Greece. No one is sure whether Aesop was a real person, but if he was, he may have been born as early as 600 B.C. One thing is certain: people have been telling fables such as this one for a long, long time.

Staging

A sawhorse, stick horse, or even two chairs or stools placed one behind the other could serve as the donkey. Father and son can interact with the donkey prop according to the indications in the script.

Vocabulary

Introduce and discuss the following words before reading the script:

clod: a dull, stupid person

dolt: a stupid, slow-witted person

fast: firmly or securely fastened

gush: to flow in plentiful quantity

hank: a loop or coil of something flexible, such as yarn or rope

jeer: to make fun of rudely; to mock or taunt

lash: to fasten or tie with a rope

prance: the lively movement of a horse

stout: sturdy or strong in body

trudge: to walk wearily or with difficulty

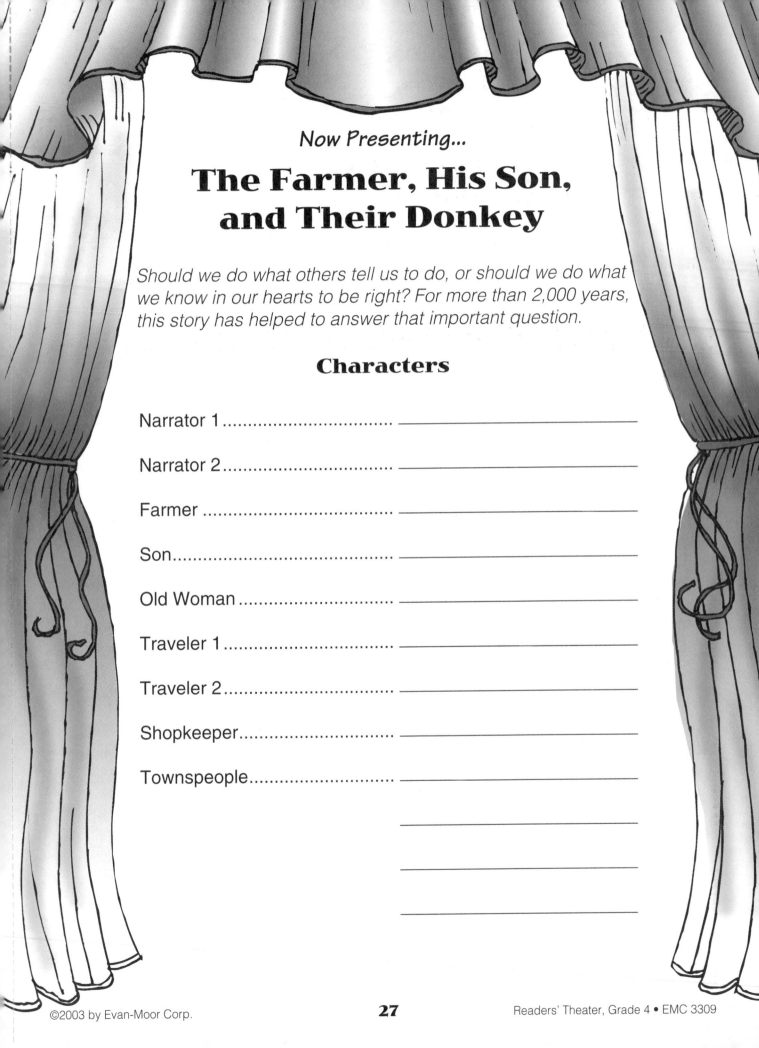

Now Presenting...

The Farmer, His Son, and Their Donkey

Should we do what others tell us to do, or should we do what we know in our hearts to be right? For more than 2,000 years, this story has helped to answer that important question.

Characters

Narrator 1 .... _____

Narrator 2 .... _____

Farmer .... _____

Son... _____

Old Woman .... _____

Traveler 1 .... _____

Traveler 2 .... _____

Shopkeeper............................. _____

Townspeople........................... _____

_____

_____

_____

The Farmer, His Son, and Their Donkey

Narrator 1: One bright day in a long ago springtime, a farmer and his son set off for the marketplace. They felt very happy to be together and they strolled along, whistling and enjoying the sunshine. Their donkey trailed contentedly behind them as they made their way over the long and dusty road to town.

Farmer and Son: *(whistling a simple tune)*

Farmer: It's a grand day to be out and about in the world, don't you think?

Son: Surely I do, Father. I can't wait to get to the marketplace. I want to buy a jam cake and a new slingshot.

Farmer: And I hope to get some fat red hens and a sack of good yellow corn to plant.

Narrator 2: And so the farmer and his son continued their journey in fine spirits, thinking good thoughts about the day ahead. The donkey ambled along behind them.

Narrator 1: After a while they came upon an old woman, hoeing the weeds in her garden by the roadside.

Farmer: *(cheerfully)* Good day, madam.

Old Woman: *(with a grumpy voice)* I will not wish you a good day, sir.

Farmer: *(confused)* And why not? What have I done to you?

Old Woman: It is not what you have done to me, sir, but what you have done to that child of yours. How dare you make him trudge through the dust while that donkey prances along without a care in the world? You should be ashamed of yourself, making the poor boy walk in this heat.

Farmer: *(nervously)* Why, yes, I see what you mean. I wonder that I did not think of it before. Here, son, climb right up on the donkey and rest your legs.

Narrator 2: Now the boy was not a bit tired, and he did not really wish to ride the donkey. But he was an agreeable lad, so he climbed up on the donkey's back, and the three continued their journey.

Narrator 1: After a while they met a pair of travelers coming along the road in their direction.

Traveler 1: Look at that rude boy, riding while his poor old father walks.

Traveler 2: What a good-for-nothing boy he must be!

Narrator 2: The harsh words stung the boy, and he jumped right down into the road.

Son: Father, you must ride. I don't mind walking.

Farmer: *(doubtfully)* I suppose you are right. Thank you, son.

Narrator 1: So with the father riding the donkey, and the boy walking along beside, the three continued their journey.

Narrator 2: After a while they came to the edge of the town. A shopkeeper stood in his doorway and watched them pass.

Shopkeeper: I have never seen such a pair of dolts! That strong little donkey can easily carry the two of you. Why does one walk when both of you could ride?

Narrator 1: The farmer and his son were both feeling a bit bewildered by this time, and only wished to be left alone, so they tried to ignore the shopkeeper. This made the shopkeeper mad, and he ran into the street.

Shopkeeper: Can't you hear me, you great selfish clod? Let your son ride with you. That donkey is a fine strong animal. It won't hurt him a bit!

Narrator 2: The farmer was upset by the shopkeeper's angry words, so he called to his son.

Farmer: Come, Son. Jump up behind me. We both can ride the rest of the way.

Narrator 2: The boy climbed up on the patient donkey behind his father, and the three continued on their journey.

Narrator 1: Very soon, they passed a group of townspeople, who began to jeer and yell.

Townspeople: What cruel people you are! Are you trying to break that poor donkey's back? Shame on you!

Narrator 2: The farmer and his son scrambled quickly down off the donkey's back and looked at each other. They did not know what to do.

Townspeople: The donkey has carried you for miles. Why don't you try carrying him for a change? *(laughing)*

Farmer: *(with frustration)* All right, all right! If it will make you happy we will carry the donkey!

Son: But Father, how will we do it? He will not like it. He will surely kick us! And he is far too heavy.

Farmer: We only need a stout pole and some rope. We can lash the donkey's feet to the pole. We can each lift one end of the pole and carry our donkey to the marketplace. We have only a short way to go now.

Son: *(doubtfully)* It might work.

Townspeople: Go find a stout pole. And bring some rope. Hurry!

Narrator 1: The townspeople rushed to their homes and quickly found a strong hickory pole and a hank of rope. They stood by and watched as the farmer and his son struggled to tie the donkey's feet to the pole.

Narrator 2: This was not an easy thing to do. No one had asked the donkey about the plan, and he clearly wanted no part of it. He thrashed and kicked and bucked and brayed. But at last he was tied fast to the pole.

Narrator 1: The farmer took one end of the heavy pole and lifted it to his shoulder. His son did likewise. With staggering steps, they continued on their journey.

Narrator 2: After a few minutes, they came to a bridge over a river. The water gushed noisily beneath the bridge. The sound terrified the poor donkey, who was feeling rather dizzy from traveling in this upside-down manner.

Narrator 1: The donkey began to struggle and kick, trying to free himself. Suddenly, the ropes broke with a snap and the poor donkey went flying over the side of the bridge and into the rushing water below.

Narrator 2: The farmer and his son dashed down to the bank of the river. But there was nothing they could do. The current was swift and deep, and the faithful donkey quickly sank out of sight.

Townspeople: Look what has happened! Look what you have done!

Farmer: *(despairingly)* Oh no! We have lost our donkey. This is awful!

Son: *(crying)* Our poor donkey has drowned. It is all our fault. We should never have listened to those foolish people!

Farmer: *(sadly)* You are wise beyond your years. I should have trusted my own heart and mind, and not the words of others.

Narrator 1: And so the farmer and his son turned sadly toward their home, having learned a painful lesson.

Farmer and Son: If you try to please everyone, you will end up pleasing no one!

Name _____

Terms from the Tale

Find the words in the Word Box that match the definitions, and then use them to complete this crossword puzzle.

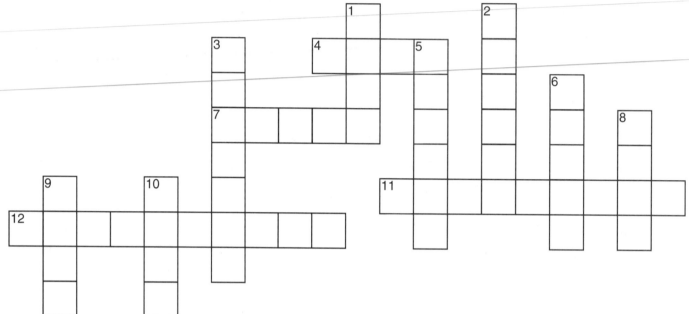

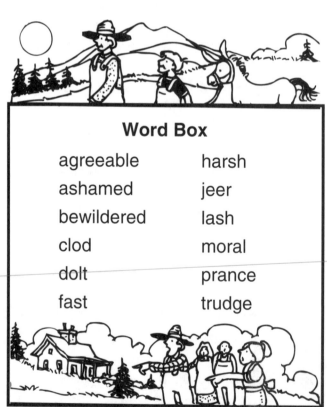

Across

4. firmly fastened
7. unpleasantly sharp or rough
11. easygoing
12. puzzled

Down

1. to tie with rope
2. a horse's lively gait
3. embarrassed
5. to walk wearily
6. the lesson in a story
8. another word for *clod*
9. to mock
10. a dull person

Word Box

agreeable	harsh
ashamed	jeer
bewildered	lash
clod	moral
dolt	prance
fast	trudge

Readers' Theater, Grade 4 • EMC 3309

Name _____

The Moral of the Story

The farmer and his son state the lesson—or moral—of this story at the end: *If you try to please everyone, you will end up pleasing no one.* Have you ever tried to please someone else, and ended up unhappy because you didn't please yourself? Tell about a time when you experienced something similar in your own life. Or, tell how you decided to follow your heart instead, and how you felt about it.

_____

_____

_____

_____

_____

_____

_____

_____

_____

_____

_____

_____

_____

_____

Name _____

Speak Your Mind,
Follow Your Heart

If the farmer and his son could start the day over again, they probably would do things quite differently. In each of the scenes below, write what the father or son would say to each person if he really spoke his mind and followed his heart.

How dare you make your poor son walk in this heat!

_____
_____
_____
_____

How can that good-for-nothing boy ride while his poor father has to walk!

_____
_____
_____
_____
_____

How foolish not to let the donkey carry you both!

_____
_____
_____
_____

How cruel you are to overload that poor donkey!

_____
_____
_____
_____

Now Presenting...

Keelboat Annie

When a power outage disrupts Crystal's entertainment plans at her slumber party, her favorite aunt, Aunt Lois, saves the day with stories of the legendary Annie Christmas.

Setting the Stage

Background

Invite students to share what they know about tall tales and the characters in them, such as John Henry, Slue-Foot Sue, and others. Be sure to point out that tall tales often take realistic elements and greatly exaggerate them to create entertaining and humorous stories.

Staging

Provide a chair for Aunt Lois. Crystal and her three friends can sit on the floor around her. Clear off an area to one side for Annie and the two bullies. Annie can wrap a piece of yarn around her neck to represent the necklace of bullies' teeth.

Vocabulary

Introduce and discuss the following words before reading the script:

incredulous: doubting; unable to believe

keel: the main timber that extends along the entire length of the bottom of a boat and supports the frame

rudder: a wide, flat, movable piece of wood used to steer a boat

taken aback: startled and confused

treacherous: giving a false appearance of safety and reliability; dangerous

tributary: a stream that flows into a larger river

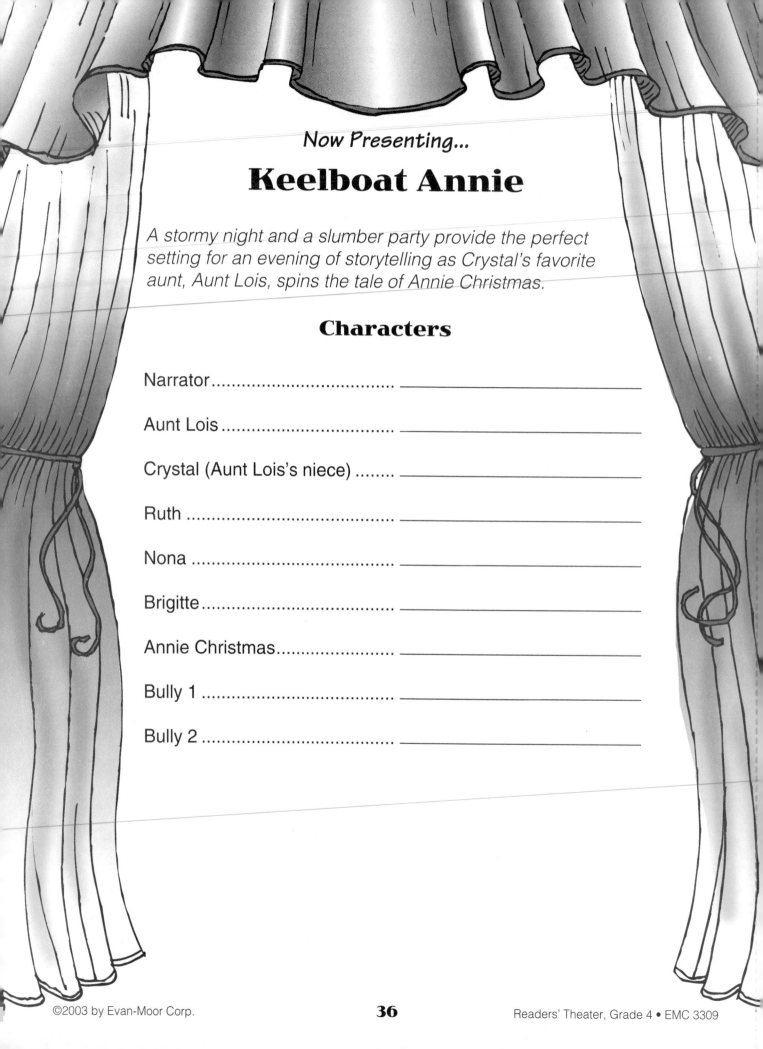

Now Presenting...

Keelboat Annie

A stormy night and a slumber party provide the perfect setting for an evening of storytelling as Crystal's favorite aunt, Aunt Lois, spins the tale of Annie Christmas.

Characters

Narrator.................................... _____

Aunt Lois .... _____

Crystal (Aunt Lois's niece) .... _____

Ruth .... _____

Nona .... _____

Brigitte.................................... _____

Annie Christmas...................... _____

Bully 1 .... _____

Bully 2 .... _____

Keelboat Annie

·················· **Characters** ··················

Narrator   Brigitte
Aunt Lois   Annie Christmas
Crystal   Bully 1
Ruth   Bully 2
Nona

Narrator: Crystal has invited her three best friends over for a slumber party. They are planning to stay up late eating popcorn and watching some of their favorite movies.

Crystal: This is going to be so much fun! I can't wait to see *The Little Dragonfly* again!

Ruth: And you know how much I love *Princess LuLing!*

Nona: *(smiling)* No bedtime, hot buttered popcorn, my favorite movies, and my best friends. What could possibly be better?

Narrator: As the girls settle down with a giant bowl of popcorn, they suddenly hear a loud BOOM! The lights go out and the room is plunged into darkness.

Nona: Oh, my gosh! They were actually right about that storm they predicted!

Ruth: I guess so! The power's out! There's no electricity at all!

Brigitte: *(making spooky sounds)* Ooooo! This could get scary!

Crystal: What are we going to do? We were going to watch movies all night! Now what do we do?

Ruth: Isn't your Aunt Lois staying with you again? I'd love to visit with her! I remember when she came to school last year and told our class all those stories about John Henry and Paul Bunyan and his big blue ox.

Nona: Yeah, and about Slue-Foot Sue and Calamity Jane!

Narrator: Suddenly, from the dark living room comes the sound of four voices, joined together in an urgent cry.

Brigitte, Crystal, Nona, Ruth: Aunt Lois!! Come here, please!

Narrator: A moment later, the living room is bathed in a warm light as Aunt Lois enters carrying a lantern.

Aunt Lois: Goodness gracious, girls. What's all the fuss?

Crystal: The electricity's out and we can't watch our movies! What are we going to do all night long?

Aunt Lois: I was wondering how long it would take before you girls started hollering for help. I think what you need is a good story about a woman who knew how to take care of herself. Keelboat Annie was more likely to help others than to need help herself—that's for certain!

Brigitte: I've never heard of Keelboat Annie. Who's she?

Aunt Lois: (incredulous) Who's Keelboat Annie? What do they teach you in school these days? Why, Keelboat Annie was the queen of the Mississippi!

Crystal: The Mississippi? Isn't that way down in the South?

Aunt Lois: Actually, child, the Upper Mississippi begins way up north in Great Lakes country, up in Minnesota.

Ruth: (amazed) No way! But it comes out in the Gulf of Mexico, in Louisiana!

Aunt Lois: I guess you *are* learning something in school after all. That mighty river actually runs right smack down the middle of the country. It seems like every little creek and stream in the land is a tributary! Why, the Mississippi gets so filled up with water that it just about spills over its banks! That mighty Mississippi can be awfully powerful—even wicked at times. You had to be mighty strong to run a keelboat on that river.

Nona: What's a keelboat? Is it like those old-fashioned riverboats?

Aunt Lois: Keelboats were much smaller and flatter, more like a barge. They were used before steamboats. A skilled keelboat captain could navigate that rushing river with nothing more than a sail, a strong hand on the rudder, and a sharp eye. To go upriver, though, a captain had to arrange for people or mules to pull the keelboat. 'Course, Keelboat Annie didn't have to hire mules. She could pull the boat herself, even if it was loaded with 200 barrels of cotton!

Brigitte: *(incredulous)* No way!

Aunt Lois: *(laughing)* Oh, Keelboat Annie wasn't your run-of-the-mill woman. Some folks say she stood a full seven feet tall, though my great-grandma—who knew Miss Annie personally—told me she wasn't more than 6 foot, 12 inches. And some folks say Keelboat Annie weighed 250 pounds of solid muscle, but my great-grandma told me she weighed in at a full 300. She said she knew this for a fact because she once saw Annie ride a seesaw with a 300-pound prize bull.

Brigitte: *(to the other girls)* Um. . . okay. . . whatever you say.

Aunt Lois: Believe what you will, but I'm telling you Keelboat Annie was one larger-than-life human being. Folks say her beautiful skin was as black as the night, and her hair was as wild as the river itself. Annie Christmas was a sight to behold! My great-grandma once saw her walk a ship's gangplank with a barrel of cotton under each arm and one on her head. Folks up and down the Mississippi admired Annie Christmas. You see, there was only one thing Miss Annie liked better than steering her boat down the most treacherous channels of the Mississippi....

Crystal: And what was that?

Aunt Lois: She loved running bullies out of town. Any time Miss Annie came ashore at a riverside town, she kept a sharp lookout for bullies. No one knows exactly why, but she just couldn't abide the idea of some tough guy picking on someone who was littler or meeker.

(Annie Christmas moves to the cleared area of the "stage." Aunt Lois continues with the story, while the action shifts to Annie and the bullies.)

Annie: This seems like a nice little town. I wonder if they've got any seesawing bulls around here?

Narrator: Two bullies walk by, eating oranges and talking loudly about their exploits.

Bully 1: I'll bet that little old lady will think twice before she goes marketing on a Wednesday again!

Bully 2: *(laughing)* You said it! I sure do love the taste of a good orange, especially if it's been snatched from an old lady!

Aunt Lois: Now, Annie could not believe what she had just heard. What kind of lowdown, no-good skunks would steal oranges from old ladies? She feared her ears were playing tricks on her, so she walked right up to those two bullies.

Annie: Excuse me, gentlemen. Did you just say that you stole those oranges from an old lady who was doing her Wednesday marketing?

Aunt Lois: The bullies were a bit taken aback at Annie's size, but, being bullies, they weren't very smart.

Bully 1: You heard what you heard, lady. This here bag of oranges was snatched right from the hands of an old woman.

Annie: *(taking a deep breath)* You're going to return those oranges.

Bully 2: *(with a wide grin)* And if we don't?

Aunt Lois: Annie was distracted for a moment by the bully's grin. She noticed his two rows of perfect teeth. Now, Annie didn't like violence, but she could defend herself. And she was mighty fond of collecting bullies' front teeth. She strung them onto a necklace that was already 10 feet long and wrapped around her neck in 10 strands.

Nona and Ruth: *(with disgust)* Ew, nasty!! Gross!

Aunt Lois: The bullies hadn't noticed her necklace because, being bullies, they weren't too sharp.

Annie: Then I'll take that bag of oranges and return it myself.

Aunt Lois: Just then, the second bully tried to sneak behind Annie, and the first bully made a terrible mistake: he actually tried to take a swing at Keelboat Annie! Annie ducked and the punch missed her, but it landed right smack in the center of the second bully's mouth. Out flew those two perfect front teeth! Annie reached down and snatched them up, knowing they would make a nice addition to her necklace. She grabbed the bag of oranges that the bullies had dropped in the scuffle. They were so busy throwing punches that they didn't notice Keelboat Annie taking off with the bag of oranges and the two perfect front teeth.

Crystal: C'mon, Aunt Lois! Do you really expect us to believe that story?

Aunt Lois: Believe what you will. But I'll tell you this: not only could Annie Christmas take care of herself just fine, she was also ready to stand up for the small and meek.

Brigitte: Just like Robin Hood!

Nona: Yeah, he stole from the rich to help the poor.

Crystal: That's right, Aunt Lois, you've told me tales about Robin Hood before. How about telling us one of those stories now?

Aunt Lois: I thought I was here on vacation! I need to get some rest, and you girls do too. Wake me up bright and early, and I'll come back and spin you another yarn. Now get to sleep!

Crystal: Good night, Aunt Lois!

Crystal, Ruth, Nona, Brigitte: And thanks for the tall tale!

Name _____

Picture This!

Review the script to find physical descriptions of Annie Christmas. Based on what you read, draw a picture of Keelboat Annie. On the lines below, list the features you included as well as the number of the page and paragraph where you found the information.

Annie Christmas

Features	Page #	Paragraph #

Name _____

Truth or Exaggeration?

As you know, tall tales include lots of exaggeration. Read each sentence below that contains information from the story. If the information is true, write a **T** in the box. If it's an exaggeration, write an **E**. Then write a true sentence that is not an exaggeration, as in the completed example.

1. Keelboat Annie could pull a boat loaded with 200 barrels of cotton.   `E`

   Keelboat Annie was a very strong woman.

2. The Mississippi River starts near the Great Lakes in Minnesota.   ☐

   _____

3. Every creek in the United States flows into the Mississippi River.   ☐

   _____

4. To go upriver, a keelboat has to be pulled by people or mules.   ☐

   _____

5. At six foot twelve, Miss Annie was 250 pounds of solid muscle.   ☐

   _____

6. Annie Christmas rode a seesaw with a 300-pound bull.   ☐

   _____

7. Keelboats were used on the Mississippi before steamboats.   ☐

   _____

8. Keelboat Annie used a sail and a rudder to guide her boat.   ☐

   _____

9. Miss Annie collected the front teeth of bullies.   ☐

   _____

Now Presenting...

An Underwater Web of Life

All living things in the mysterious depths of the sea must eat in order to live, just like the creatures on land. By giving its life, each creature helps sustain other life-forms in the sea, as underwater animals are connected in a wondrous web of life.

Setting the Stage

Background

Introduce or review with students the basic concepts of food webs in nature. Remind them that all animals must eat in order to survive, and the animals in the ocean are no exception. You may need to remind students that some animals get their energy from plants (which get their energy from the sun), while others get their energy by eating other animals. Tell students that in this poetic performance, they will present an undersea food web, where creatures from tiny plankton to majestic killer whales all play a part in the cycle of life.

Staging

You might wish to have students create posters of each of the "characters" to display behind the readers during the performance of this script.

Encore

Students may use the viewers they make (see pages 50 and 51) to guide them in describing an underwater web of life, or in a creative retelling of this script.

Vocabulary

Introduce and discuss the following words before reading the script:

codfish: a type of fish usually found in northern seas

diatoms: microscopic algae that live in colonies and serve as a food source for many forms of marine life

herring: a small, silvery fish found in northern seas

killer whale: a very large marine mammal of the dolphin family, mainly black with white spots, that preys on large fish, seals, and whales

krill: a small, shrimplike crustacean

nutrients: an ingredient or substance in a food that provides nourishment

orca: another name for a killer whale

seal: a marine mammal with a doglike head, torpedo-shaped body, and four flippers; it usually lives in cold or temperate waters

squid: a long, slender, carnivorous marine mollusk with eight arms and two long tentacles

zooplankton: microscopic animal life-form that floats and drifts in the ocean and serves as a food source for many forms of marine life

Readers' Theater, Grade 4 • EMC 3309

Now Presenting...

An Underwater Web of Life

The sea is filled with a stunning variety of animals. Each of them must eat in order to live, and in dying, each also helps give life to others. Like animals on land, undersea creatures are connected in a complex web of life.

Characters

The Sea .... _____

The Diatoms............................... _____

_____

The Zooplankton .... _____

_____

The Krill .... _____

_____

The Herring .... _____

The Squid................................... _____

The Codfish............................... _____

The Seal..................................... _____

The Orca .... _____

Readers' Theater, Grade 4 • EMC 3309

An Underwater Web of Life

···················· **Characters** ····················

The Sea   The Squid
The Diatoms   The Codfish
The Zooplankton   The Seal
The Krill   The Orca
The Herring

···

The Sea: This is the sea, where the tide rises and falls, high and low, high and low. Where the waves break on the shore, in and out, in and out. Round and round, again and again, morning and evening, forever and ever.

The Diatoms: These are the diatoms, millions and billions. Tiny plants making energy from the sun.

The Sea: Here in the sea, where the tide rises and falls, high and low, high and low. Where the waves break on the shore, in and out, in and out. Round and round, again and again, morning and evening, forever and ever.

The Zooplankton: These are the zooplankton, strange to behold. Odd little creatures in all sorts of shapes.

The Diatoms: They eat the diatoms, millions and billions. Tiny plants making energy from the sun.

The Sea: Here in the sea, where the tide rises and falls, high and low, high and low. Where the waves break on the shore, in and out, in and out. Round and round, again and again, morning and evening, forever and ever.

The Krill: These are the krill, like wriggling shrimp . . .

The Zooplankton: . . . who eat the zooplankton, strange to behold. Odd little creatures in all sorts of shapes . . .

The Diatoms: . . . who eat the diatoms, millions and billions. Tiny plants making energy from the sun.

The Sea: Here in the sea, where the tide rises and falls, high and low, high and low. Where the waves break on the shore, in and out, in and out. Round and round, again and again, morning and evening, forever and ever.

The Herring: These are the herring, slim little fish . . .

The Krill: . . . who eat the krill, like wriggling shrimp . . .

The Zooplankton: . . . who eat the zooplankton, strange to behold. Odd little creatures in all sorts of shapes . . .

The Diatoms: . . . who eat the diatoms, millions and billions. Tiny plants making energy from the sun.

The Sea: Here in the sea, where the tide rises and falls, high and low, high and low. Where the waves break on the shore, in and out, in and out. Round and round, again and again, morning and evening, forever and ever.

The Squid: This is the squid, with tentacles long . . .

The Herring: . . . who eats the herring, slim little fish . . .

The Krill: . . . who eats the krill, like wriggling shrimp . . .

The Zooplankton: . . . who eat the zooplankton, strange to behold. Odd little creatures in all sorts of shapes . . .

The Diatoms: . . . who eat the diatoms, millions and billions. Tiny plants making energy from the sun.

The Sea: Here in the sea, where the tide rises and falls, high and low, high and low. Where the waves break on the shore, in and out, in and out. Round and round, again and again, morning and evening, forever and ever.

The Codfish: This is the codfish, spotted and green . . .

The Squid: . . . who eats the squid, with tentacles long . . .

The Herring: . . . who eats the herring, slim little fish . . .

The Krill: . . . who eats the krill, like wriggling shrimp . . .

The Zooplankton: . . . who eat the zooplankton, strange to behold. Odd little creatures in all sorts of shapes . . .

The Diatoms: . . . who eat the diatoms, millions and billions. Tiny plants making energy from the sun.

The Sea: Here in the sea, where the tide rises and falls, high and low, high and low. Where the waves break on the shore, in and out, in and out. Round and round, again and again, morning and evening, forever and ever.

The Seal: This is the seal, gleaming and sleek, with shining coat and playful ways . . .

The Codfish: . . . who eats the codfish, spotted and green . . .

The Squid: . . . who eats the squid, with tentacles long . . .

The Herring: . . . who eats the herring, slim little fish . . .

The Krill: . . . who eats the krill, like wriggling shrimp . . .

The Zooplankton: . . . who eat the zooplankton, strange to behold. Odd little creatures in all sorts of shapes . . .

The Diatoms: . . . who eat the diatoms, millions and billions. Tiny plants making energy from the sun.

The Sea: Here in the sea, where the tide rises and falls, high and low, high and low. Where the waves break on the shore, in and out, in and out. Round and round, again and again, morning and evening, forever and ever.

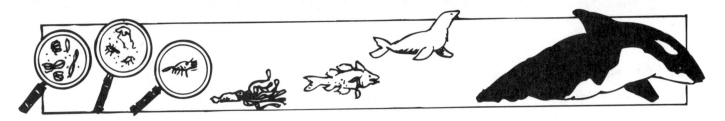

The Orca: This is the orca, the killer whale, all beauty and power in black and white . . .

The Seal: . . . who eats the seal, gleaming and sleek . . .

The Codfish: . . . who eats the codfish, spotted and green . . .

The Squid: . . . who eats the squid, with tentacles long . . .

The Herring: . . . who eats the herring, slim little fish . . .

The Krill: . . . who eats the krill, like wriggling shrimp . . .

The Zooplankton: . . . who eat the zooplankton, strange to behold. Odd little creatures in all sorts of shapes . . .

The Diatoms: . . . who eat the diatoms, millions and billions. Tiny plants making energy from the sun.

The Sea: Here in the sea, where the tide rises and falls, high and low, high and low. Where the waves break on the shore, in and out, in and out. Round and round, again and again, morning and evening, forever and ever.

The Diatoms and Zooplankton: This is the mighty orca, come to his end. His body gives back to the sea, providing the nutrients that diatoms and zooplankton need to live and to give life to their fellow creatures. And so their lives go on . . .

The Sea: . . . here in the sea, where the tide rises and falls, high and low, high and low. Where the waves break on the shore, in and out, in and out. Round and round, again and again, morning and evening, forever and ever.

 Readers' Theater, Grade 4 • EMC 3309

A Circle of Life

You will need:

- 2 copies of page 50, copied on card stock
- 1 copy of page 51
- scissors
- glue
- paper fastener
- crayons or markers (optional)

Directions:

1. Cut out both circles along the dotted line.

2. On one circle only, cut out the section labeled "1."

3. Color the pictures on page 51 and write the name of each life-form.

4. Cut out the pictures and glue them in order onto the whole circle. Begin by gluing the picture of the sea and the sun in the section labeled "1."

5. Place the circle with the cut-out section over the circle with the pictures. Then push a paper fastener through the center of both circles.

6. Spin it to show each scene as you describe the underwater web of life.

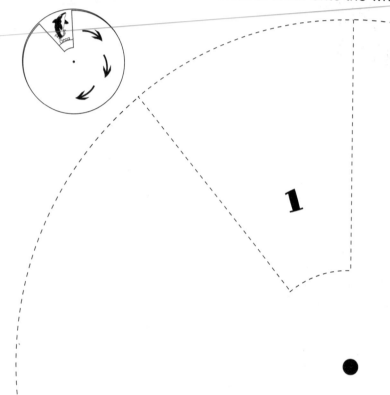

1

Readers' Theater, Grade 4 • EMC 3309

A Circle of Life

Name _____

Alike and Different

The **orca**, or killer whale, is a large marine mammal. Mammals are warmblooded. They have lungs and breathe air by surfacing above the water. Mammals give birth to live young. They produce milk to feed their young. Adult orcas are predators—they hunt for food in the sea. Orcas are excellent swimmers. Their dorsal fins are the biggest in the animal kingdom.

The **codfish** is a fish. It has scales and fins. It is coldblooded. It uses gills to breathe oxygen underwater. The codfish lays millions of eggs each year. Most of the eggs are eaten by other fish in the ocean. Often, as few as two baby codfish will grow to adulthood out of these millions of eggs! Codfish eat other animals.

Use this Venn diagram to show how orcas and codfish are similar and different.

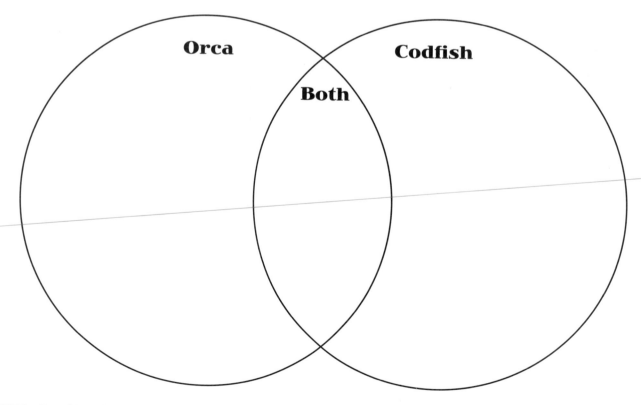

Orca   **Both**   **Codfish**

Readers' Theater, Grade 4 • EMC 3309

Now Presenting...

How Coyote Brought Fire to the People
A Native American Legend

In this traditional American Indian tale, the master trickster, Coyote, steals fire from magical beings on a mountaintop and brings it to humankind.

Setting the Stage

Background

Guide the class in a discussion of trickster characters in folklore. Some students may be familiar with the fox in Aesop's fables, or with Brer Fox in traditional African American stories. You may need to tell students that in many Native American cultures, the coyote—like the fox—is known as a clever trickster. There are countless stories of his exploits. Versions of the tale of how Coyote stole fire are told in tribes throughout North America. This script is adapted from a Karok story. (The Karok lived along the Klamath River in an area that today is part of California and Oregon.)

Staging

Divide the staging area into three parts: the village, the woodland grove, and the mountain of the Fire Beings.

You might wish to have students create posters of each of the "characters" to display behind the readers during the performance of this script.

Vocabulary

Introduce and discuss the following words before reading the script:

compassionate: feeling or showing pity or sympathy toward another

detect: to discover or notice someone or something

fragile: physically weak or delicate

frigid: extremely cold

grove: a group of trees with open ground below them

singe: to burn the tips of hair

yelp: a short, sharp cry or bark, often in pain

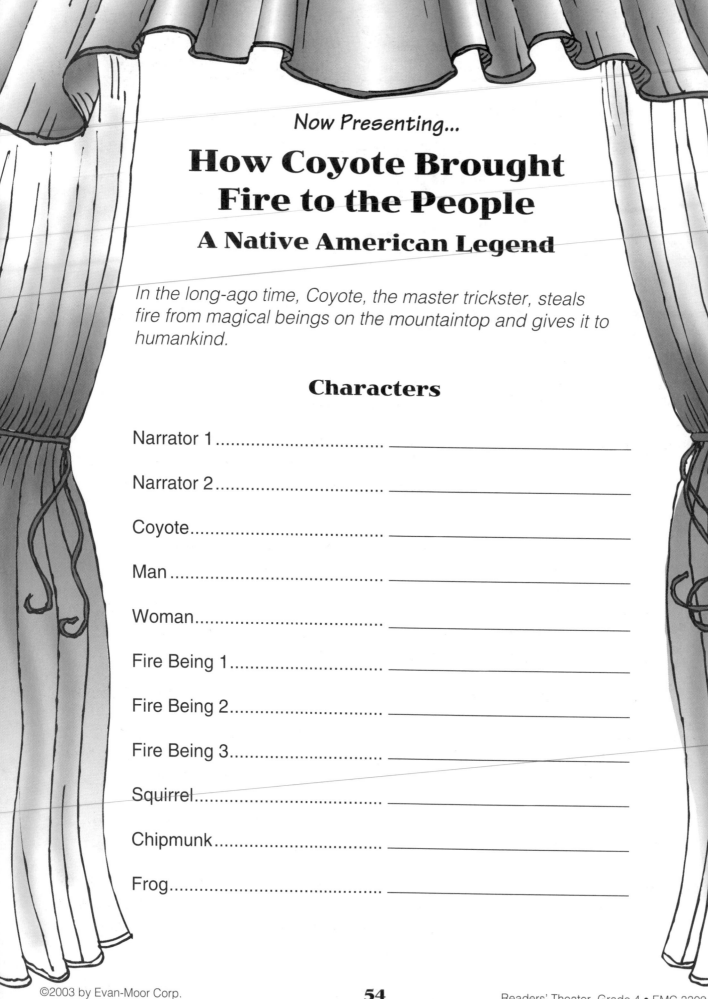

Now Presenting...

How Coyote Brought Fire to the People

A Native American Legend

In the long-ago time, Coyote, the master trickster, steals fire from magical beings on the mountaintop and gives it to humankind.

Characters

Narrator 1.................................. _____

Narrator 2.................................. _____

Coyote...................................... _____

Man.. _____

Woman..................................... _____

Fire Being 1............................... _____

Fire Being 2............................... _____

Fire Being 3............................... _____

Squirrel..................................... _____

Chipmunk.................................. _____

Frog.. _____

How Coyote Brought Fire to the People
A Native American Legend

·············· **Characters** ··············

Narrator 1   Fire Being 2
Narrator 2   Fire Being 3
Coyote   Squirrel
Man   Chipmunk
Woman   Frog
Fire Being 1

Narrator 1: In the long-ago time, human beings were new in the world. With the eyes of children, they observed the workings of the earth. They marveled at how day became night, and how night turned back into day.

Narrator 2: In the springtime, they welcomed the warmth of the sun, and in the summer they danced in fields of wildflowers.

Narrator 1: But in the autumn, the humans grew worried. They saw that the days grew shorter and the nights grew longer. In the mornings, frost covered the ground and tender plants withered and died.

Man: The nights are getting colder and colder. Soon the snows will come.

Woman: You and I are strong. We can survive the hardships of the snows. But I am worried about our baby. He is so very small. I can wrap him in furs and animal skins, but is he strong enough to survive?

Man: I, too, am worried. There are many in the village who are very old. I am afraid that they will suffer greatly when the snows come.

Narrator 1: At that very moment, Coyote was walking by the village on his way to the woodland grove. He was going to meet his friends Frog, Chipmunk, and Squirrel. He paused for a moment and listened to the words spoken by Man and Woman.

Narrator 2: Coyote was a compassionate animal. When he heard the man and woman talk of the hardships of winter, his heart was moved.

Coyote: I have never thought much about the coming of winter. My fur grows thick and warm in the cold of winter. But these human beings have no warm fur to protect them from the bitter cold.

Narrator 2: Coyote trotted on to the grove. There he met his friends.

Coyote: I have just come from the village of the humans.

Chipmunk: You went to the village? But the humans are such strange creatures. They know so little of the world.

Squirrel: And they know nothing of our language. I have often tried to speak to them, but they do not respond.

Frog: The humans are indeed strange. I have seen them at the edge of the pond, gazing at the water for the longest time. They seem to be staring at their own reflections! I say those humans are best left alone.

Coyote: But Frog, I heard the woman speak of the coming snows. She was worried about her young one. And the man spoke of how the old ones suffer with the cold. Friends, I fear for the humans . . . but I think I may know how to help these fragile creatures. *(pausing)* Do you know of the Fire Beings on the mountaintop?

Frog: I have heard stories of the three ancient beings. It is said that they dwell at the top of the highest mountain, guarding a burning light that gives off heat all through the day and night.

Coyote: The stories are true, Frog. I have been to that mountaintop, and I have seen the burning light. It is called "fire," and it may help the humans survive the winter. I must find a way to bring fire to the village!

Narrator 1: Chipmunk, Squirrel, and Frog knew that Coyote was the cleverest of all the animals, but they were worried about their friend. As Coyote headed off toward the mountain, they decided to follow him.

Narrator 2: When Coyote neared the camp of the Fire Beings, he crouched down behind some thick bushes so he wouldn't be detected. He did not know that Chipmunk, Squirrel, and Frog were also hiding nearby. Through the brush, Coyote spotted the Fire Beings.

Fire Being 1: Ah . . . the warmth of this fire feels so good! Soon it will be winter, but we will stay warm through the long frigid nights because we alone know the secret of fire.

Fire Being 2: *(greedily)* Yes, we alone hold the secret.

Narrator 1: Darkness fell. As Coyote watched, two of the Fire Beings retired to their tents. One stayed up to guard the fire. Hour after hour passed, but still the Fire Being remained awake by the fire pit.

Narrator 2: At dawn, the Being who had stared into the glowing fire all through the night stood up. It stretched its arms to the sky and yawned. Slowly it made its way to its tent. Coyote noticed that one of the other tents was shaking. The Being inside was waking up, and soon it would emerge to guard the fire. This was the chance Coyote had hoped for.

Narrator 1: Coyote leapt over the bushes and ran as quickly as he could toward the fire.

Fire Being 3: What's that noise?

Fire Being 2: What's happening?

Narrator 2: The three Fire Beings jumped from their tents just as Coyote grabbed a bit of the fire.

Coyote: *(laughing)* Ha, ha! Soon the humans will know the precious secret of fire, and the young ones and elders will no longer have to suffer with the cold snows of winter!

Fire Being 1: *(screaming)* Catch him! Catch him! He has our fire!

Narrator 1: The three magical beings ran after Coyote. One reached out its hand and grabbed Coyote's tail.

Fire Being 1: I've got him! I've got him!

Narrator 1: Coyote yelped as the Fire Being's hand singed the tip of his tail. He flung the fire as far away from him as he could. To this day, the tips of coyotes' tails are as white as ash where the fur was singed.

Narrator 2: Squirrel saw Coyote throw the fire, and she ran as fast as she could in order to catch it before it hit the ground.

Squirrel: I'll place the fire on my back so I can run more quickly.

Narrator 1: Squirrel put the fire on her back and ran as fast as she could. The fire hurt so badly that her tail curled up and back. You may have noticed that squirrels' tails still curl that same way to this day.

Squirrel: Chipmunk, Chipmunk! Catch!

Narrator 2: Squirrel threw the fire to Chipmunk.

Chipmunk: I've got it! I've got it!

Narrator 1: As Chipmunk turned to run, a Fire Being blocked his path.

Fire Being 1: Not so fast, thief.

Narrator 2: The Fire Being reached out its hand and tried to grab Chipmunk, but he was too quick. Chipmunk darted away just as the Fire Being's claws scratched at his back. You may have noticed, even today, that chipmunks have three white stripes down their backs.

Chipmunk: Frog, Frog! Catch!

Frog: I've got it! I've got it!

Narrator 2: Frog turned to jump away, but a Fire Being stepped on his tail. Frog pulled with all his might. He pulled until his eyes bulged and his tail tore off. You may have noticed that to this day frogs still have no tails, and their eyes still bulge out of their heads.

Frog: Help! Help! What shall I do with this fire?

Narrator 1: Frog threw the fire to Wood, and Wood swallowed it. The three Fire Beings drew together around Wood, but they did not know how to get the fire out.

Fire Being 1: Wood, pretty Wood. Give us back our fire. It is rightfully ours.

Fire Being 2: Wood, pretty Wood. Come with us to the mountaintop and we will make you one of us.

Fire Being 3: Wood, pretty Wood. We must have the fire. Tell us what you desire, and it will be yours.

Narrator 2: But Wood had seen how the Fire Beings had scratched and clawed at the other animals, and he did not trust them. Finally, when the Fire Beings saw that they could not get the fire out of Wood, they gave up and returned to their mountaintop.

Narrator 1: But clever Coyote *did* know how to get the fire out of Wood. He took Wood to the village, and he showed the human beings how to rub two dry sticks together to start a fire.

Narrator 2: And the people were filled with joy.

Man: No longer will our grandparents suffer through the long cold nights of winter. With Coyote's gift of fire, we can feel the warmth of the sun day or night, winter or summer!

Woman: Our children will grow and thrive and enjoy many an evening around the glow of the fire.

Narrator 1: Coyote watched as the people rejoiced, and he was glad.

Name _____

Energy Alternatives

Long ago, humans used fire to help them meet some of their basic needs. Today, humans have several options to help them meet those same needs.

- In Column 1, list at least three ways that fire was used by early humans.
- In Column 2, list alternatives to fire used by modern people for the same purposes.
- In Column 3, list the advantages of the modern alternatives to fire.
- In Column 4, list the disadvantages of the modern alternatives to fire.
- Use the lines below the chart to write your conclusions about the best sources of energy today. Give reasons to support your conclusions.

How Fire Was Used Long Ago	Alternatives to Fire Used Today	How Are Today's Alternatives Better?	How Are Today's Alternatives Worse?

_____

_____

_____

_____

Name _____

Fact or Fiction?

The tale "How Coyote Brought Fire to the People" explains how human beings learned about fire. It also explains why animals have certain characteristics. Review what the script says about each animal. Then use these T-charts to write information from the play about each animal. Write information that is make-believe under **Fiction**, and true information under **Fact**. The first one has been started for you.

 **Coyote**

Fiction	Fact
Coyotes talk to humans and animals.	Coyotes howl.

 **Squirrel**

Fiction	Fact

 **Chipmunk**

Fiction	Fact

 **Frog**

Fiction	Fact

Now Presenting...

The Sager Children

After a difficult westward journey on the Oregon Trail, a family of seven boys and girls is welcomed into their new home at a frontier mission.

Setting the Stage

Background

Let students know that this script is based on the true story of the Sager family, who headed west on the Oregon Trail in the spring of 1844. Along the way, a daughter was born to Henry and Naomi—already the parents of six other children. Tragically, both parents died of illness later on the journey, leaving other members of the wagon train to care for their orphaned children. They took the Sager children to the Whitman Mission in present-day Washington. There, Narcissa and Marcus Whitman took in all seven of the youngsters and raised them as their own children.

You may prefer not to tell students that this peaceful time did not last long. Three years later, the Whitmans, John and Francis (Frank) Sager, and some other settlers were killed during an Indian attack. The Sager girls were held captive for over a month, during which time Louise Sager died of illness. Henrietta, the baby, died at the age of 26, but the remaining Sager girls—Catherine, Elizabeth, and Matilda—had numerous children and lived long and happy lives.

Staging

The narrators may choose to stand apart from the other characters, who can occupy a large, open space. You may wish to provide a baby doll bundled in cloth for the final tableau.

Encore

You and your students may wish to learn more about the Whitman Mission and the Sager children by visiting the Whitman Mission National Historic Site on the Web (www.nps.gov/whmi/home.htm).

Vocabulary

Introduce and discuss the following words before reading the script:

forlorn: lonely and sad

grief: a feeling of deep suffering and sadness, often caused by loss or misfortune

hardship: a difficult situation that is hard to bear

harmony: peaceful, friendly relationships

loyal: faithful to people or ideas to whom you have made a commitment

mission: the home and workplace of those who are sent to other lands to teach and convert others to their religion

territory: a large area of land; a region

weep: to express grief or sorrow by crying and wailing

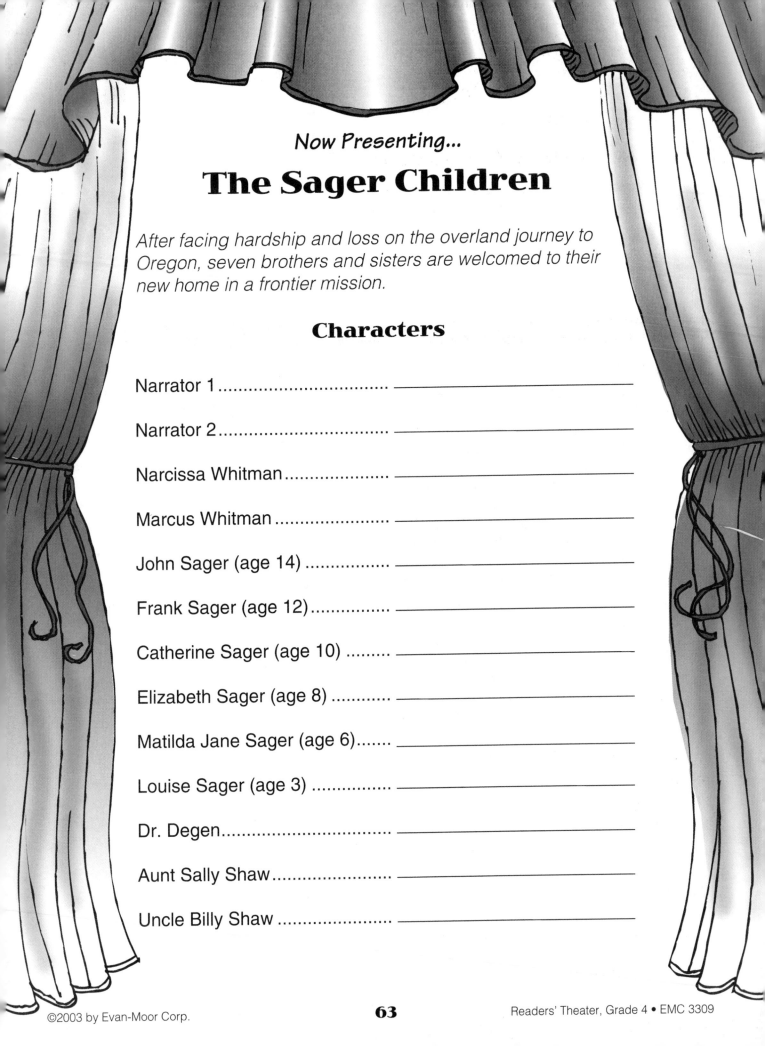

Now Presenting...

The Sager Children

After facing hardship and loss on the overland journey to Oregon, seven brothers and sisters are welcomed to their new home in a frontier mission.

Characters

Narrator 1 .... _____

Narrator 2 .... _____

Narcissa Whitman .... _____

Marcus Whitman .... _____

John Sager (age 14) .... _____

Frank Sager (age 12) .... _____

Catherine Sager (age 10) .... _____

Elizabeth Sager (age 8) .... _____

Matilda Jane Sager (age 6) .... _____

Louise Sager (age 3) .... _____

Dr. Degen .... _____

Aunt Sally Shaw .... _____

Uncle Billy Shaw .... _____

 Readers' Theater, Grade 4 • EMC 3309

The Sager Children

······················· **Characters** ·······················

Narrator 1
Narrator 2
Narcissa Whitman
Marcus Whitman
John Sager
Frank Sager
Catherine Sager

Elizabeth Sager
Matilda Jane Sager
Louise Sager
Dr. Degen
Aunt Sally Shaw
Uncle Billy Shaw

Narrator 1: Marcus and Narcissa Whitman were missionaries who traveled to the Oregon territory by covered wagon in 1836. They built a home for themselves, along with a church and a school.

Narrator 2: At first, Marcus and Narcissa spent their time trying to teach the local Indians about Christianity. But the Whitmans soon saw that the Indians' way of life was coming to an end. They realized that the Indians would need to learn the ways of the white settlers. It was more important, they believed, to teach the Indians how to farm and how to live in harmony with the newcomers.

Narrator 1: White settlers were streaming into the country. The Oregon Trail passed right by the door of the Whitman Mission. More and more, the Whitmans' time was taken up with tending to the needs of the settlers.

Narrator 2: Let's peek in on the Whitmans one late October day in 1844.

Narcissa: *(humming, pantomiming cooking)*

Marcus: Narcissa, come take a walk with me. I have some important news to tell you.

Narcissa: Of course, Marcus. Let me just put this bread in the oven. What has happened? What is the news?

Marcus: A rider stopped by a few minutes ago. He told me that a wagon train is on its way here.

Narcissa: *(laughing)* That is hardly news, Marcus! It seems a wagon train full of hungry people arrives at our doorstep nearly every day. I think I should get back to my baking if that is your news!

Marcus: *(seriously)* This wagon train is different. It is bringing a family of seven children. The mother and father both died on the journey. The children have nowhere to go. We have been asked to take them in.

Narcissa: Oh my! Seven children? How old are they? How can we make room for them? Oh, Marcus, this is terrible news indeed! Oh the poor, poor children. What shall we do?

Marcus: The two oldest are boys, near grown. They will be a big help here at the mission. The next four are girls from ten to about three years of age. The youngest is an infant girl, born last May, along the trail. I think it is asking too much of you to take her.

Narcissa: No, Marcus, she is the one I want most of all. And she will help to bind us together as a family. We must take the baby. *(sighing)* We must take them all.

Marcus: You may be right. But I worry that you will wear yourself out. Already you have so much to do, so many to care for.

Narcissa: As you already said, Marcus, the boys can help. And the older girls too. Anyway, we have no choice. We cannot turn them away. We had better get ready to make them welcome.

Narrator 2: And so the Whitmans prepared for the arrival of their new children. Meanwhile, out on the trail, the children were being well cared for.

Narrator 1: The captain of the wagon train, William Shaw, and his wife Sally were great friends to the children. The children trusted them and called them "Uncle Billy" and "Aunt Sally." Along with kindly Dr. Degen, they watched over the Sagers and did all they could to help the forlorn children.

John: *(angrily)* I don't want to go to the Whitmans! I want to go find some land of our own. That's what Papa wanted us to do.

Uncle Billy: I know it is hard to give up your father's dream, John. But for now, we must think of the girls. They are too little to face more hardship. They need a home. Try to be patient.

Frank: We promised Ma that we would take care of the girls and keep the family together. If the Whitmans will take us, I think we must go there, at least for now.

Dr. Degen: It is the wisest thing, but I know it is difficult for you all. Your sorrow is so fresh, and you are so far from home.

Louise: *(crying)* I want Mama. I want Mama.

Catherine: Shh, now. I know it's hard. But we must be brave.

Elizabeth: Yes, Mama said we should take care of each other. You will be all right, Louise. We are here. We will stay with you.

Aunt Sally: Come and sit on my lap for a while, Louise.

Matilda Jane: Will the Whitmans be nice to us, Aunt Sally?

Aunt Sally: Oh, my dear, how can they help but love such wonderful children as you are? Of course, they will be nice to you. They will give you a good home. Try not to worry, Matilda Jane.

Narrator 2: But it was hard for the children not to worry. The last weeks of travel were difficult. The children were ragged and dirty and worn out from grief and the long journey. They wondered about the place they would soon call home. Would they be welcome there? Would they be happy?

Narrator 1: When they neared the mission, Aunt Sally said good-bye to the children. Uncle Billy and Dr. Degen drove the Sager children and their few belongings to the mission house.

Catherine: Dr. Degen, I am so nervous!

Dr. Degen: Take a deep breath. It's going to be fine.

Narrator 2: As the children huddled shyly together, Uncle Billy knocked on the door of the two-story house. A kind-looking woman opened the door.

Uncle Billy: Mrs. Whitman, your children are here!

Narcissa: *(smiling)* Welcome, children! Come in, come in! You must be exhausted. Here, let me give you a hand with your things.

Children: *(crying)* Good-bye, Uncle Billy. Good-bye, Dr. Degen.

Narcissa: Poor children, it is no wonder that you weep. You have been through so much. Come along now, come inside and rest. Try to give your dear friends a smile to remember you by.

Children: Good-bye, good-bye! We will miss you.

Dr. Degen: *(sniffling)* Good-bye, children. Be good.

Uncle Billy: *(wiping his eyes)* We will come to see you when we are settled. Take care of yourselves. Good-bye, for now.

Narrator 1: As Mrs. Whitman led the children into the house, Mr. Whitman walked up to the house from the barn.

Marcus: You showed great kindness to those poor children.

Uncle Billy: They are wonderful children. Thank you so much for taking them all in. It was their parents' last wish that they remain together.

Marcus: We will keep them through the winter. If they are not happy, we will bring them to you. But they shall be together.

Uncle Billy: I can't thank you enough. Sally and I would have kept them ourselves had we a home. We are so grateful to you for your kindness. You won't be sorry that you have chosen to open your home to them.

Marcus: I am already sure of that. Is the baby here too?

Uncle Billy: Not yet. She is with a family that is a few days back on the trail. Some of the good women of the wagon train are taking turns caring for her. She should be here any day.

Narrator 1: As Uncle Billy and Dr. Degen rode off to join the rest of their group, Mr. Whitman went into the house to greet his new family.

Narrator 2: A few days later there was knock at the door. Matilda ran to open it. Standing there was a small woman holding a bundle of rags. As Mrs. Whitman approached the door, she thrust the bundle into her arms and hurried away.

Narcissa: *(joyfully)* Oh! It's the baby!

Louise: The baby! The baby is here!

Catherine: *(with excitement)* Our baby sister is finally here!

Elizabeth: At last, we are all together.

John: Just as Ma and Pa wanted us to be.

Frank: Now, we're really a family again.
(All Sager children and Whitmans stand together in a tableau.)

Narrator 1: This is where we will leave the brave and loyal Sager children, gathered around their baby sister in their new home. For the first time in many months, they feel safe and at peace, happy to be together at last.

Narrator 2: There would be more tragedy and danger in the years to come, but the long, sad journey of the Sager children had come to an end. They had indeed found a new home in the West.

Name _____

Dear Diary . . .

Imagine that you are Frank or Catherine Sager. You are keeping a diary during your westward journey on the Oregon Trail. Write an entry that tells how you feel after learning that you are to be taken in by Narcissa and Marcus Whitman at their mission in the Oregon Territory.

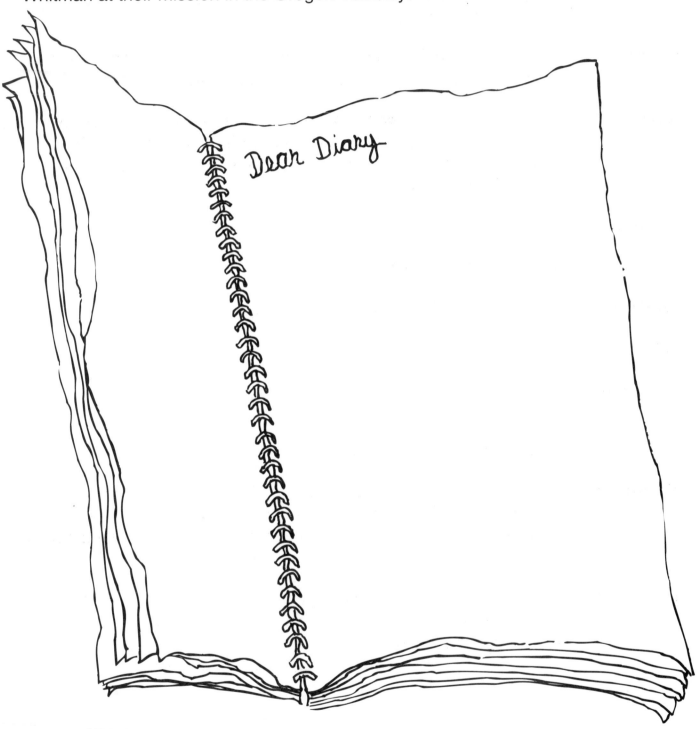

Dear Diary

Name _____

Say It with Feelings!

Each scrambled word names a feeling. Unscramble each of the jumbled words, and then use it in a sentence.

anxious forlorn	brave concerned	hopeful grateful	heartbroken joyful

rolfnor ◯ ◯ ◯ ◯ **◯** ◯ ◯

pufeloh ◯ ◯ **◯** ◯ ◯ ◯

tagfruel ◯ ◯ ◯ ◯ **◯** ◯ ◯

evarb ◯ ◯ ◯ **◯** ◯

folyuj **◯** ◯ **◯** ◯ ◯ ◯

axsionu ◯ ◯ ◯ ◯ **◯** ◯ ◯

dreccenno ◯ ◯ ◯ ◯ ◯ ◯ ◯ ◯ **◯**

earthknober ◯ ◯ ◯ **◯** ◯ ◯ ◯ ◯ ◯ ◯ ◯

Unscramble the letters in the dark circles above to spell the answer to this question:
How do the Sager children feel when the play is over?

◯ ◯ ◯ ◯ ◯ ◯ ◯ ◯ ◯

Readers' Theater, Grade 4 • EMC 3309

Now Presenting...

The Timekeepers

An old watchmaker falls asleep at his workbench and has a dream. In his dream, people from the distant past appear to share with him their ways of keeping time.

Setting the Stage

Background

Ask students to brainstorm ways to tell time. In addition to using clocks, guide them toward an understanding of how they can make educated guesses about time by determining the position of the sun and by recognizing the activities of the day. Make sure they are aware that ancient peoples told time by a variety of methods, including sundials and sand and water clocks.

Staging

Divide the staging area into two parts: the watchmaker's shop and the land of dreams.

Encore

Your students may enjoy experiencing other ways to measure time. They can make a simple sundial by downloading directions and patterns from a NASA Web site (http://kids.msfc.nasa.gov/Earth/Sundials/SundialMake.asp).

Vocabulary

Introduce and discuss the following words before reading the script:

artifice: a clever, skillfully made resource to meet a particular need

chastise: to scold

disdain: to look down upon; to treat as unworthy

dubious: feeling doubt

etch: to make a design by pressing sharply into a surface

feat: a remarkable accomplishment or deed

intricate: full of elaborate detail

sophisticated: very complex

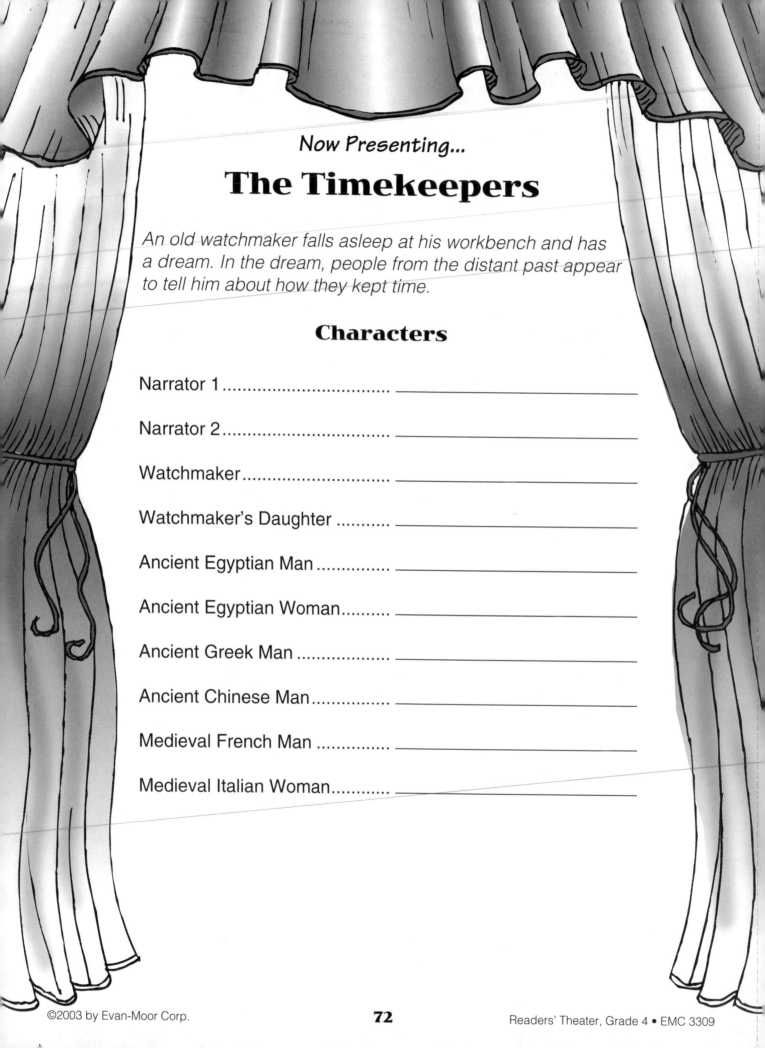

Now Presenting...

The Timekeepers

An old watchmaker falls asleep at his workbench and has a dream. In the dream, people from the distant past appear to tell him about how they kept time.

Characters

Narrator 1.................................. _____

Narrator 2.................................. _____

Watchmaker.............................. _____

Watchmaker's Daughter .... _____

Ancient Egyptian Man .... _____

Ancient Egyptian Woman.......... _____

Ancient Greek Man .... _____

Ancient Chinese Man................ _____

Medieval French Man .... _____

Medieval Italian Woman............ _____

The Timekeepers

······················· **Characters** ·······················

Narrator 1
Narrator 2
Watchmaker
Watchmaker's Daughter
Ancient Egyptian Man

Ancient Egyptian Woman
Ancient Greek Man
Ancient Chinese Man
Medieval French Man
Medieval Italian Woman

Narrator 1: In a little house in a little town lived a little old man.

Narrator 2: The little old man was a watchmaker. He took great pride in making timepieces by hand, fitting and assembling the tiny parts that kept track of seconds, minutes, and hours.

Narrator 1: Long into the night, the watchmaker would work and work, until each watch was perfect.

Narrator 2: The watchmaker's daughter would often chastise the old man for working too hard. Late one night she entered the old man's workshop, where she found him hunched over the small gears and springs of a new watch.

Watchmaker's Daughter: Father! What are you doing? Do you know it's after 11 p.m.? Why do you work so hard making watches by hand? Don't you know that no one wants such timepieces anymore? They want cheap plastic watches made by machines.

Watchmaker: My dear, do you know how amazing watches are? Each one is a work of art and science. Think about the people who will depend on this watch. Think about the mother who will use this watch to know exactly when to expect her children to return from school. Think about the father who will depend on this watch to know exactly what time his daughter's softball game begins. *(with disdain)* Plastic watches! Time is too important to leave to chance.

Watchmaker's Daughter: *(sighing)* Father, you are hopeless. The world is moving forward, and you are stuck in the past.

Narrator 1: The watchmaker's daughter left the old man alone in his workshop.

Watchmaker: *(to himself)* Perhaps my daughter is right. Perhaps I am stuck in the past. The world seems to be moving so quickly these days.

Narrator 2: The watchmaker put his head down on the workbench. Soon he was snoring quietly.

Watchmaker: *(talking in his sleep)* Time . . . moving too fast . . .

Narrator 1: The old man began to dream. In his dream he was approached by a man wearing the clothes of ancient Egypt.

Ancient Egyptian Man: *(to Watchmaker)* So, old man, you think that time is moving too fast, eh? It might surprise you to learn that there really is no such thing as time. That which we call time is simply an artifice, designed for human convenience.

Watchmaker: What do you mean? I build watches. I construct tiny gears that keep track of each second, of each minute. Of course there is such a thing as time!

Ancient Egyptian Man: There is indeed day and night, and one day passes into the next. But that which we refer to as time was created by human beings so that we would know when to plant our fields and when to harvest our crops. Before watches, we told time by the sun and the moon and the stars. In fact, we Egyptians invented the 24-hour day.

Watchmaker: *(looking dubious)* What do you mean?

Ancient Egyptian Man: Actually, we didn't truly think of a day as consisting of 24 hours. Rather, we divided the day into two 10-hour blocks. We then added two hours for dawn and two hours for dusk. Our word for hour meant "priest's duties." Telling time was one of the many duties assigned to our priests.

Watchmaker: But without watches, how could you know when an hour passed?

Ancient Egyptian Man: We created devices that measured the shadows cast by the sun. At night we watched for certain stars to rise on the eastern horizon. As each star appeared, a new hour began.

Narrator 2: Suddenly, a woman wearing the clothes of ancient Egypt appeared in the dream. She was holding a bent T-shaped object made of wood.

Ancient Egyptian Woman: *(holding up the object)* This is the sun clock we used for telling time. You can see that the crossbar of the "T" sticks up. The long part of the "T" rests on the ground and has marks on it. In the morning, we would face the clock toward the east. As the sun crossed the sky, the shadow cast by the crossbar would move down the long bar. We could tell the hour by seeing which mark the shadow touched. At noon we would face the clock toward the west. Once again, the shadow would travel across the marks on the long bar. You can see that this tool is not as advanced as your mechanical watches, but it informed us of the passing of time.

Watchmaker: Ingenious! You could track the hours with the sun!

Ancient Egyptian Woman: That is correct. And at night our priests would record the appearance of stars on sophisticated charts.

Narrator 1: The watchmaker put his head back down on his workbench. The ancient Egyptian man and woman disappeared, but he was soon greeted in his dream by a man wearing the clothes of ancient Greece.

Ancient Greek Man: Watchmaker! I understand you are impressed by the sun clocks of the Egyptians. Know that we Greeks also kept time with devices that tracked the motion of the sun.

Watchmaker: Really? I had no idea that those in the ancient world were so inventive!

Ancient Greek Man: Indeed. Our sun clocks were made of curved pieces of pottery. We inserted a pointer at the center, and we etched lines into the clay. As the shadow of the pointer moved across the pottery, the lines told us the time.

Watchmaker: I never knew humans could tell time without the benefit of intricate machinery!

Narrator 2: Suddenly, a man wearing the clothes of ancient China appeared.

Ancient Chinese Man: You speak of intricate machinery. You have seen nothing until you have seen the intricate water clocks of old China.

Watchmaker: Water clocks? How can water be used to tell time?

Ancient Chinese Man: Our water clocks were very elaborate. But I will tell you about the very simplest of them so that you will understand. Our simplest water clocks were nothing more than clay pots with lines etched inside. Water was filled to the top line. When a person was ready to keep track of the passing time, a plug was pulled at the bottom of the pot. The water trickled out slowly through a tiny hole in the bottom. As the water in the pot went down, the lines on the inside of the pot showed the hours.

Narrator 1: The watchmaker put his head back down on his bench. The ancient Greek man and the ancient Chinese man disappeared. In their place appeared a man from medieval France and a woman from medieval Italy.

Medieval French Man: Watchmaker! You wish to know of time. In medieval France, we tracked the passing of time with sand. Surely you have heard of an hourglass! An hourglass consists of two glass bulbs connected by a short, narrow tube. One of the bulbs is filled with fine sand. When the hourglass is turned, the sand drains out of the top bulb and into the bottom one. When all of the sand has drained, an hour has passed.

Medieval Italian Woman: In Milan we have a large bell in the town square. Our keenest scientists have devised a machine that strikes the bell upon the hour. For example, if it is 3 o'clock, we hear the bell being struck three times. Everyone in town knows the hour.

Watchmaker: Time is truly a feat of human understanding. And human creativity has given us ingenious ways to measure time!

Narrator 2: The old man put his head back down on his bench. The next thing he knew, he was being awakened by his daughter.

Watchmaker's Daughter: *(shaking the old man's shoulders)* Father, wake up! Father! Do you wish to sleep away the whole morning? Do you know what time it is?

Watchmaker: Do I know what time it is? Sit down, my dear, and let me tell you about time!

Name _____

Telling Time

Write the name of each type of clock. Then list the advantages and disadvantages of each type of clock.

Ancient Clocks	Advantages	Disadvantages
_____		
_____		
_____		

If you had to use one of these clocks to tell time daily, which would you choose? Why? Write your answer and give your reasons below.

_____

_____

_____

78

Name _____

Time Flies

Practice your time-telling skills with the exercises below.

1. Tameka rolls out of bed at 6:00 a.m. It takes her 5 minutes to put on her robe and walk downstairs. It takes her another 15 minutes to eat a bowl of oatmeal and drink a glass of milk. She then takes a shower that lasts 20 minutes. Tameka spends 10 minutes brushing her teeth and drying her hair, and another 10 minutes getting dressed. It takes her 5 minutes to put on her coat and leave the house. Her walk to the bus stop takes 5 minutes, and she spends 10 minutes waiting for the bus. What time is it when Tameka finally gets on the bus?

_____

2. At 3:15 p.m., Raul heads to the baseball field for practice. It takes him 5 minutes to walk from the locker room to the dugout. He realizes he has forgotten his mitt, so he has to go back to the locker room. What time is it when Raul returns to the dugout?

_____

3. Betsey knows she is going to be late for her audition for the school play. It is 3:00 p.m., and she lives an hour from school. She still has to get dressed, which will take her 10 minutes. Her brother is going to give her a ride, but his old car always takes 5 minutes to start. Also, he needs to get gas on the way, and that will take another 5 minutes. Auditions start promptly at 3:45 p.m. How late will Betsey be?

_____

4. Bob helps his dad at the furniture store after school. He leaves school at 3:30 p.m. and spends 20 minutes walking to the store. He then heads for the workroom where he fritters away 15 minutes drinking a soda and eating a snack. He then spends 45 minutes doing his homework. At what time does Bob start helping his dad?

_____

Now Presenting...

Sojourner Truth:
A Life Devoted to Justice

Although she was born into slavery, Sojourner Truth grew up with a powerful sense of justice. As a freed woman, Truth spoke out for women's rights at a time when women had little voice in public affairs, and women of African descent had even less power.

Setting the Stage

Background

Explain to students that the movement for women's rights in the United States grew out of the abolitionist movement—the movement to end the enslavement of Africans and their descendants. Remind students that prior to the ratification of the Nineteenth Amendment in 1920, women did not have the right to vote.

Tell students that Sojourner Truth, the subject of this play, was a historical figure who was born into slavery with the name Isabella Baumfree (BOME free). She endured countless hardships before gaining her freedom, and went on to become famous as a powerful speaker for abolition and women's rights. Some of the words in this play were actually spoken by Sojourner Truth when she addressed the Women's Rights Convention in Akron, Ohio, in 1851. That speech became quite famous, and has come to be known as "Ain't I a Woman?"

Staging

Divide the stage into two areas: one where the scenes from Truth's early life take place, and the other representing the setting at the Women's Rights Convention. For the convention setting, arrange several chairs in a semicircle around a podium, where Truth can stand to speak the words from her famous "Ain't I a Woman?" speech.

Vocabulary

Introduce and discuss the following words before reading the script:

abolition: doing away with something, especially with the institution of slavery

intercede: to plead or make a request on behalf of somebody else

justice: fairness

out of kilter: wrong; not as it should be

sojourner: a traveler who stays for a short visit before moving on

suit: a legal action undertaken in an effort to receive justice from a court of law

Now Presenting...

Sojourner Truth:
A Life Devoted to Justice

Although she was born into slavery, Sojourner Truth grew up with a powerful sense of justice. As a freed woman, Truth spoke out for women's rights at a time when women had little voice in public affairs, and women of African descent had even less power.

Characters

Narrator 1 .... ——————————————

Narrator 2 .... ——————————————

Isabella Baumfree .... ——————————————
(Sojourner Truth as a young girl)

Betsy (Isabella's mother) .... ——————————————

Isaac Van Wagener .... ——————————————

John Dumont .... ——————————————

Sojourner Truth .... ——————————————

Frances Gage .... ——————————————
(presiding officer of the Women's Rights Convention)

Male Minister 1 .... ——————————————

Male Minister 2 .... ——————————————

Male Minister 3 .... ——————————————

Bethany .... ——————————————

Nadine .... ——————————————

 Readers' Theater, Grade 4 • EMC 3309

Sojourner Truth:
A Life Devoted to Justice

··· **Characters** ·······························

Narrator 1   Sojourner Truth
Narrator 2   Male Minister 1
Isabella Baumfree   Male Minister 2
Betsy   Male Minister 3
Isaac Van Wagener   Nadine
John Dumont   Bethany
Frances Gage

Narrator 1: In 1797 Sojourner Truth was born into slavery in New York State. She was given the name Isabella Baumfree.

Narrator 2: Now, Baumfree is an unusual name. It comes from the Low Dutch language spoken in New York, and it means "tree." Isabella's father was very tall, and he stood very straight. That's why he was called Baumfree.

Narrator 1: Isabella's mother was named Betsy, but she was known by her nickname: Mau-mau-Bett. When she was very young, Isabella would sit with her mother under the trees, and together they would gaze up at the stars.

Betsy: *(to Isabella)* Remember Isabella, whenever times get tough, just look up at the stars. The heavens are bigger than all of us. Looking at the stars reminds us that there's a plan to the world, though we may not understand it.

Isabella: But Mama, why can't we understand it? Why must life be so hard?

Betsy: I don't know, child. But just remember: Look at the stars when you need the strength of the heavens. That strength is always there for you.

Narrator 2: Soon Isabella would learn what her mother meant. She was about to face one of the greatest hardships of her life.

Narrator 1: Isabella's beloved mother died, and not long after—when she was just nine years old—she was sold away from her family. She was made to work very hard, but when she was able, Isabella would glance up at the night sky and remember her mother's words.

Isabella: *(gazing at the stars)* I'm trying to be strong, Mama. But I miss you so much, and I feel so very alone.

Narrator 2: Two years later, when she was 11, Isabella was sold again, this time to a fisherman.

Narrator 1: For the next 18 months, Isabella was made to work very hard, and she missed her father terribly.

Isabella: It isn't right that I should be away from my father. It isn't right that people can buy and sell other people. I'm trying so hard to be strong, but I know in my heart that this just isn't right.

Narrator 2: Isabella had a strong sense of right and wrong. Later in her life, she spoke out against injustice. Now, she was just a little girl kept in slavery.

Narrator 1: Before she turned 13, Isabella was sold again, this time to a man named John Dumont. She spent many years working in his fields, milking his cows, weaving his cloth, cooking for him, and caring for his children.

Narrator 2: During those years, Isabella married Thomas, another of Mr. Dumont's slaves. In time, they had five children together. Even though there were moments of happiness, life as a slave was never easy.

Narrator 1: But then, in 1827, when Isabella was about 30, the state of New York passed a bill to grant freedom to slaves of Isabella's age. When Mr. Dumont refused to grant Isabella her freedom as the law provided, she turned once again to the heavens to pray for strength and guidance.

Isabella: Lord, help me be strong. Help me do the right thing. I have this baby daughter in my arms, and I can't stand to see her raised up in slavery.

Narrator 2: Then Isabella decided to do something very brave. She decided to take her infant child and just walk away from John Dumont.

Narrator 1: She walked and walked until she came upon a house owned by Mr. and Mrs. Van Wagener, two very kind people.

Narrator 2: It wasn't long, though, before John Dumont came looking for her.

John Dumont: So you've run away from me, Isabella.

Isabella: No, sir. I did not run away. I walked away by daylight.

John Dumont: You know you must go back with me.

Isabella: No, I won't go back with you.

John Dumont: Well, I shall take the child.

Isabella: No, sir. You shall not.

Isaac Van Wagener: *(interceding)* Now see here. I don't believe in slavery, and I've never bought nor sold another human being. But rather than have you take Isabella and her baby back by force, why don't I purchase her services from you?

John Dumont: *(stroking his chin)* Hmmm. That might work. Let's see. She owes me another year of work. If you pay me $20 for Isabella and $5 for the child, then they can stay here with you.

Narrator 1: For the next two years, Isabella was employed by the Van Wageners. While there, she found out that one of her sons, Peter, had been sold out-of-state illegally. She filed a suit in court, and she won—the first black woman to sue a white man and win!

Narrator 2: You see, Isabella had not forgotten what she had learned about right and wrong.

Narrator 1: The years passed, and Isabella continued working for justice—for abolition and for women's rights. When she was 46 years old, she adopted the name Sojourner Truth.

Narrator 2: Sojourner Truth traveled from city to city, speaking about justice. In 1851 she attended the Women's Rights Convention in Akron, Ohio.

Narrator 1: Little did she know that on that day she would make a speech that would be remembered even to this day.

(Frances Gage, Sojourner Truth, the ministers, Bethany, and Nadine move to the semicircle and podium.)

Frances Gage: *(at the podium)* Ladies and gentlemen! Order, please! We are about to begin. As you know, we are here at this convention to discuss the issue of women's rights. Why is it that we live in a free land, but women are prohibited from voting?

Minister 1: *(laughing)* You ask, "Why?" The answer is obvious. Men have a superior intellect, that's why.

Minister 2: *(also laughing)* Besides, Christ was a man. That obviously means that men are to be favored.

Minister 3: *(more seriously)* Now, now . . . Ladies are to be protected from the unpleasantness of public life. They are to be treated with courtesy. They are to be helped into carriages, and they are to be taken to all the best places.

Narrator 2: At this, Sojourner Truth rose and approached the podium. You remember, she had a very strong sense of right and wrong, and she could not bear to be silent when faced with injustice.

Bethany: Mrs. Gage! Don't let that woman speak!

Nadine: Mrs. Gage! You can't let her speak! People will confuse the issue of women's rights with abolition! Don't let her speak.

Frances Gage: *(sternly)* If Sojourner Truth wants to address this Convention, she may.

Narrator 1: Sojourner Truth stood at the podium and looked out at the crowd. In a powerful voice, she began to speak.

Sojourner Truth: Well, children, where there is so much racket, there must be something out of kilter….

Narrator 2: Sojourner pointed to one of the ministers.

Sojourner Truth: That man over there says that women need to be helped into carriages, and lifted over ditches, and to have the best place everywhere. Nobody helps me any best place. And ain't I a woman?

Narrator 1: Sojourner's voice rose as she stood up straight and tall.

Sojourner Truth: Look at me! Look at my arm.

Narrator 2: Sojourner bared her right arm and flexed her powerful muscles.

Sojourner Truth: I have plowed, I have planted, and I have gathered into barns. . . And ain't I a woman? I could work as much, and eat as much as a man—when I could get it—and bear the lash as well! And ain't I a woman? I have borne children and seen most of them sold into slavery, and when I cried out with a mother's grief, none but Jesus heard me. And ain't I a woman?

Narrator 1: The women in the audience began to cheer wildly. Sojourner pointed to another minister.

Sojourner Truth: He talks about this thing in the head. What's that they call it?

Frances Gage: *(whispering)* Intellect.

Sojourner Truth: That's it. What's intellect got to do with women's rights or black folks' rights? And that man over there *(pointing)*. He says that women can't have as much rights as men, 'cause Christ wasn't a woman. Well . . . where did your Christ come from? From God and a woman! Man had nothing to do with him.

Narrator 2: The crowd erupted in applause. Sojourner took her seat while the audience clapped and cheered.

Narrator 1: For the remainder of her life, Sojourner continued working tirelessly for justice—for women's rights, for abolition, and for an end to capital punishment. She died at her home in Michigan at the age of 86.

Name _____

Right or Wrong?
True or False?

Read the following statements carefully. If the statement is true, write a **T** in the blank. If it is false, write an **F** and rewrite the statement to make it true.

1. _____ Isabella's father was named Baumfree because he was short.

_____

2. _____ When Isabella was 12 years old, she was sold away from her family.

_____

3. _____ Isabella had a very strong sense of right and wrong.

_____

4. _____ Isabella had five children.

_____

5. _____ Isabella ran away from Mr. Dumont in the middle of the night.

_____

6. _____ Isaac Van Wagener paid Mr. Dumont for a year of Isabella's work.

_____

7. _____ When she was 46 years old, Isabella adopted the name Sojourner Truth.

_____

8. _____ In 1851 Sojourner Truth attended the National Abolitionists Convention in Akron, Ohio.

_____

9. _____ Frances Gage did not allow Sojourner Truth to speak at the Convention.

_____

10. _____ As an adult, Sojourner Truth worked tirelessly for justice—for women's rights, for abolition, and for an end to capital punishment.

_____

Name _____

A Tribute to Truth

Sojourner Truth had a deep belief in justice and freedom for all. Imagine that you have been invited to submit a design for a monument honoring the memory of Sojourner Truth. What would your monument look like? What words or message would you include in your monument? Use this space to design your monument to Sojourner Truth and all that she stood for.

_____

_____

_____

_____

_____

Now Presenting...

How Animals Got Their Beautiful Coats

This classic Zulu folktale from southern Africa tells the story of how animals got their coats.

10 parts

Setting the Stage

Background

Lead students in brainstorming the reasons that animals look the way they do. Make sure that students come to an understanding of the relationship between animals and their environment. For example, some animals have stripes for camouflage, while others have spots or can even change color. Some have thick fur to keep them warm, while others have feathers to help them fly.

Tell students that the script they are about to hear is based on a traditional Zulu story that explains why animals' coats are colorful and attractive.

Staging

Arrange the stage area in two sections: the campfire and the jungle.

Vocabulary

Introduce and discuss the following words before reading the script:

dangle: to sway to and fro from a hanging position

exquisite: having great and delicate beauty

obstinate: stubborn; not easily persuaded

stoke: to feed a fire with fuel

suspend: to hang from above

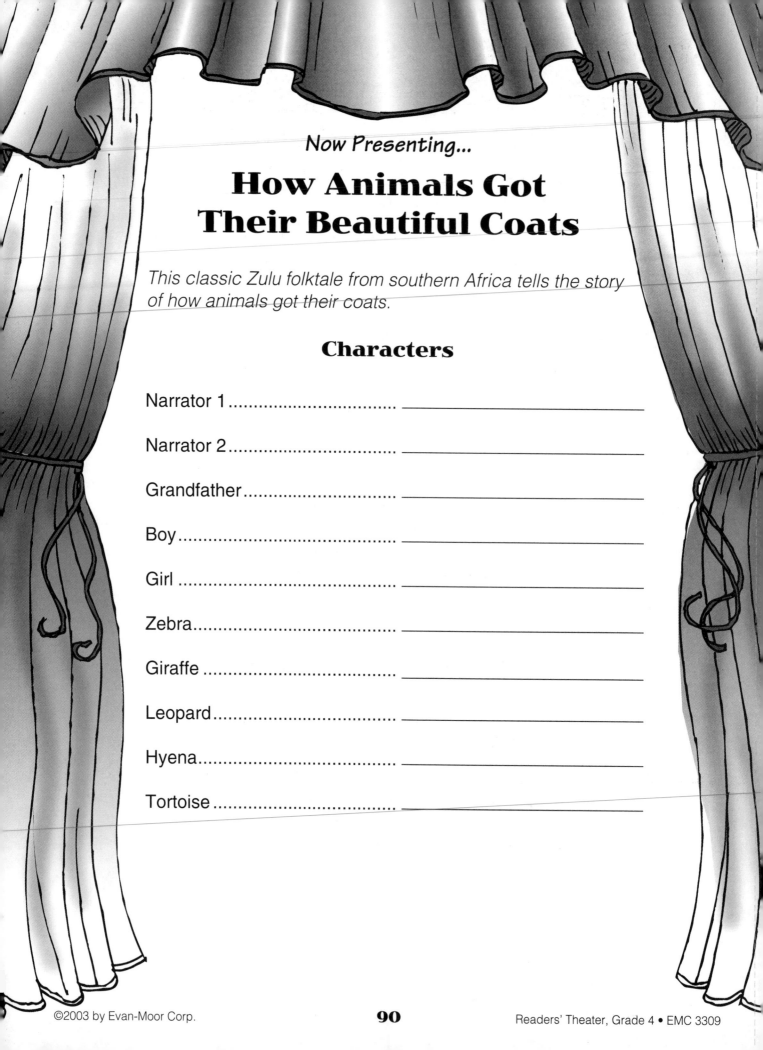

Now Presenting...

How Animals Got
Their Beautiful Coats

This classic Zulu folktale from southern Africa tells the story of how animals got their coats.

Characters

Narrator 1 .... _____

Narrator 2 .... _____

Grandfather .... _____

Boy .... _____

Girl .... _____

Zebra.. _____

Giraffe .... _____

Leopard... _____

Hyena.. _____

Tortoise .... _____

 Readers' Theater, Grade 4 • EMC 3309

How Animals Got Their Beautiful Coats

.... **Characters** ....

Narrator 1	Zebra
Narrator 2	Giraffe
Grandfather	Leopard
Boy	Hyena
Girl	Tortoise

Narrator 1: A long time ago, in a small village in southern Africa, there lived an old man.

Narrator 2: The old man had two grandchildren: a girl and a boy.

Narrator 1: Night after night, the boy and the girl refused to go to sleep until their grandfather told them a story. They would sit by the fire long after everyone else had gone to bed, waiting to hear some tale of adventure or some legend of their tribe.

Grandfather: *(to the boy and girl)* Children, all the people in the village are asleep. Why do you stay awake night after night?

Boy: *(smiling)* Grandfather, you know we cannot sleep until you tell us a story.

Girl: *(smiling)* Grandfather, you are the best storyteller in the village. The fire is warm, and we are tired, but we must hear a story.

Grandfather: *(sighing)* Children, I have told you all the stories I know. I have told you of the tricky hyena, and I have told you of the royal lion. I have shared with you stories of how the world came to be and stories of our ancestors. I know no other tales. Now go to bed.

Boy: *(stubbornly)* We will not go to bed until we hear a story.

Narrator 2: The old man sighed because he knew his grandchildren were obstinate. Although it frustrated him sometimes, he was glad to know that they had minds of their own.

Narrator 1: The old man stoked the fire and settled back on his mat.

Grandfather: Children, have you ever wondered how the animals got such beautiful coats?

Girl: What do you mean? They have the coats that they have. There is nothing to wonder about.

Grandfather: Ah, but they didn't always have the coats that they do now. Back in the beginning, before humans walked the plains, all the animals had coats of a dull brown.

Boy: You mean the tall giraffe was brown? And the leopard?

Girl: *(laughing)* Really, grandfather. You can do better than that.

Grandfather: It's true. All the animals were the same ugly color of mud. Zebra, Giraffe, Leopard, and Tortoise were all the same dreary brown. Hyena was brown too. But Hyena was also mean. He liked to pick on other animals, and he usually picked on animals that were smaller than he was.

Boy: Hyena sounds like a bully.

Grandfather: Indeed he was, child. Indeed he was.

(The action moves to the jungle area of the stage.)

Tortoise: *(to himself)* How difficult it is to make my way along this jungle path. The leaves are so deep in some places that I can barely push my way through. But I must return home.

Narrator 2: Just then, Hyena jumped right into Tortoise's path.

Hyena: *(snidely)* Well, well, well . . . if it isn't Tortoise. Where are *you* off to in such a hurry?

Tortoise: If you must know, I'm on my way home. Now, if you'll excuse me.

Narrator 1: Tortoise attempted to go around Hyena, but Hyena snatched him up in his mouth. Hyena was very fast.

Narrator 2: Hyena thought it would be funny to play a trick on Tortoise. He tied a vine to Tortoise's leg and dangled him from a tree limb. He really *was* a bully.

Hyena: *(laughing)* You look so funny suspended from that tree! When the breeze blows, you swing back and forth.

Tortoise: Hyena! Please help me down. I can feel the vine slipping, and I'm afraid that I'll fall.

Narrator 1: But Hyena didn't hear Tortoise because he was laughing too loudly. He ran off and left poor Tortoise hanging from the tree limb.

Narrator 2: Just then, Leopard came along the path.

Leopard: Why, Tortoise! Whatever are you doing?

Tortoise: Please, Leopard, help me down. I can feel the vine slipping, and I'm afraid that I'll fall.

Leopard: Of course I'll help you, Tortoise. Hold on.

Narrator 1: Leopard climbed the tree and untied the vine from around Tortoise's leg. Carefully Tortoise climbed onto Leopard's back, and the two made it safely down from the tree.

Tortoise: Thank you, Leopard. You saved my life. Now I would like to do something special for you.

Narrator 2: Tortoise made a silvery yellow paint from flower petals. He colored Leopard from head to toe, and then he added spots.

Tortoise: Now you are beautiful. When the other animals see you, they will know you have done a good deed.

Narrator 1: Leopard went on his way. Soon he ran into Zebra.

Zebra: *(to Leopard)* My, what a beautiful coat. Where did you get it?

Leopard: My friend Tortoise gave it to me. If you ask him nicely, perhaps he will give you a fine new coat as well.

Narrator 2: So Zebra went to Tortoise and asked him for a new coat.

Tortoise: *(to Zebra)* Of course I will make a pretty coat for you, but I will have to create some new colors.

Narrator 1: Tortoise painted Zebra with beautiful black and white stripes. Then he polished Zebra's hooves until they shined.

Narrator 2: Zebra thanked Tortoise, and he went on his way. Soon he ran into Giraffe.

Giraffe: *(to Zebra)* My goodness, Zebra! Where did you get that lovely coat?

Zebra: My friend Tortoise gave it to me. If you ask him nicely, perhaps he will give you a fine new coat as well.

Narrator 1: So Giraffe went to Tortoise, and he asked him for a new coat.

Narrator 2: Tortoise mixed an exquisite cream color for Giraffe, and he topped it off with reddish spots.

Giraffe: *(to Tortoise)* Thank you, Tortoise. My new coat is magnificent, indeed.

Narrator 1: Giraffe went on his way. Soon he ran into Hyena.

Hyena: Well, well, well. Look at Giraffe and his fancy new coat. Tell me, where did you get it?

Giraffe: My friend Tortoise gave it to me. Perhaps if you ask him nicely, he will give you a fine new coat as well.

Narrator 2: Hyena went to Tortoise, but he had no intention of asking him nicely for anything.

Hyena: *(to Tortoise)* I have seen the beautiful coats you have made for the other animals. You had better make one for me too, or I'll eat you!

Tortoise: Hyena, I will have to give you a haircut before I color your coat.

Narrator 1: Tortoise picked up a knife. He held Hyena steady with one hand, while he cut Hyena's fur with the other. But Tortoise did not cut neatly. He cut Hyena's hair so that it was long and shaggy in some areas, and short and stubby in others. He then brushed Hyena's hair so that it stood up in some places, and laid flat in others.

Narrator 2: Then Tortoise mixed all the colors together before smearing them on Hyena's coat. He then stood back and looked at Hyena.

Hyena: Well, is my coat beautiful?

Narrator 1: Tortoise saw that Hyena's coat was all blotchy. He was a mix of colors: white, gray, and brown. His fur was uneven and ugly.

Tortoise: Your new coat suits you, Hyena.

(The action returns to the fireside.)

Grandfather: To this day, Hyenas have messy fur. That way everyone who sees them will know that they are mean and unpleasant animals.

Boy: *(yawning)* Thank you, Grandfather. That was a wonderful story.

Girl: *(yawning)* Yes, thank you, Grandfather. Now we can go to sleep.

Grandfather: Off to bed now, children. And have pleasant dreams of Tortoise, Leopard, Zebra, and Giraffe.

Name _____

Compare This Pair

Use the chart below to help you compare and contrast Tortoise and Hyena.

- First, focus on three attributes—or characteristics—such as personality, physical features, attitude, or any others.

- Use the columns below each animal to describe their attributes.

- Then use the ideas from the chart to write a paragraph comparing Tortoise and Hyena. Describe their similarities and differences and your opinion of each animal.

	Tortoise	**Hyena**
Attribute 1		
Attribute 2		
Attribute 3		

_____

_____

_____

_____

Name _____

The Moral of the Story

Many traditional stories from Africa and all over the world are designed to teach a lesson about how to live. The lesson in a story is called its **moral**. What do you think is the moral of "How Animals Got Their Beautiful Coats"? Write the moral below, and then explain the lesson of this story in your own words.

The moral of the story is: _____

_____

_____

_____

_____

To me this means: _____

_____

_____

_____

_____

_____

_____

Now Presenting...

The Chance of a Lifetime

In this modern fairy tale, a young girl uses her head to make her dream come true.

7 parts

Setting the Stage

Background

Introduce the concepts of chance, probability, and luck by flipping a coin. Ask students to name the two possible outcomes: heads or tails. Explain that the chance (or probability) of the coin coming up heads is 50:50 for each flip of the coin. Therefore, the outcome of any particular flip cannot be predicted accurately, except by a lucky guess.

Ask students to consider whether they might predict the outcome of 100 coin flips with greater accuracy. Why might this be so? You may need to explain that the outcome of 100 flips is probably going to be very close to 50:50, because the chance that the coin will come up heads is equal to the chance that it will come up tails on every throw. Allow students to experiment by working with partners to flip a penny 100 times and tally their results. Chances are, each pair will have results that are very close to 50:50.

Staging

Arrange a table and chairs to represent Carrie's humble cottage. Another part of the stage could represent the castle, where King Archibald could be seated in a special chair.

Vocabulary

Introduce and discuss the following words before reading the script:

abacus: a frame that holds balls strung on wire, used for calculating

algebra: a type of mathematics that uses letters and symbols in calculating quantities

area: the amount of surface within a specified range

calculus: in mathematics, a method of calculating and reasoning

curtsey: a greeting offered by a girl or woman, made by bending the knees and bowing

geometry: in mathematics, the study of the relationships of lines, surfaces, and solids in space

perimeter: the measurement of the outline of a closed figure

trigonometry: a type of mathematics that deals with the relations of the sides and angles of triangles

The Chance of a Lifetime

In this modern fairy tale, a young girl uses her head to make her dream come true.

Characters

Narrator 1 .... _____

Narrator 2 .... _____

King Archibald .... _____

Carrie .... _____

Carrie's Mother .... _____

Carrie's Father .... _____

Page .... _____

The Chance of a Lifetime

.... Characters ....

Narrator 1   Carrie's Mother
Narrator 2   Carrie's Father
King Archibald   Page
Carrie

Narrator 1: Long ago, in the faraway land of Tallysum, there lived a very smart teenager named Carrie. Carrie loved mathematics of all kinds. Algebra, trigonometry, calculus . . . Carrie studied them all.

Narrator 2: In her spare time, Carrie liked to play geometry games. She would wander through the village, taking measurements and finding the perimeters and areas of her neighbors' houses and gardens.

Narrator 1: One day, Carrie was sitting outside her family's cottage with her abacus, enjoying the last of the sunshine. Her mother came to the door and called her inside for dinner.

Narrator 2: Carrie went inside and joined her parents at the rough table in their small, cramped cottage.

Carrie's Mother: Here is a nice potato stew, ready for us to eat.

Carrie: *(sighing)* All right, Mother.

Carrie's Mother: What's wrong, darling? Don't you like potato stew?

Carrie: Of course, Mother. Though it would be nice to have something else once in a while.

Carrie's Mother: Ah, yes, I know, dear. But your father and I are very poor and I suppose we must count ourselves lucky to have food of any kind.

Carrie: It isn't the stew.

Carrie's Father: Well, what then? You look troubled.

$$24 \times 2 + 36 - 5 + 10 =$$

Carrie: Oh, Father, you know how I long to study at the Castle of Knowledge. The Master of All Knowledge, Ultimo the Math Wizard, is the most respected genius of the land.

Carrie's Father: *(sadly)* My good daughter, never in all my years could I collect enough money to pay for studies at the Castle of Knowledge. I'm afraid that you must set that dream aside.

Carrie: Yes, Father. I know it is foolish, but I keep hoping that something will happen . . . something to make my dream come true.

Carrie's Mother: Hold on to your hopes, dear. Who knows what might come to pass.

Narrator 1: Weeks passed. Then, one day while Carrie was hanging out the wash and estimating the number of square inches in each sheet and towel, her mother came running up the road from the village. She was waving a long printed scroll in her hand.

Carrie's Mother: *(yelling)* Carrie! Look, look! Can you believe your eyes? Look, look!

Carrie: Calm down, Mother, and let me see. What are you talking about?

Narrator 2: Carrie took the scroll from her mother's hands and read it.

Carrie: *(reading)* "Announcement: A Contest of Wits—Answer three questions and the prize will be yours! Grand Prize: A full four-year scholarship to the Castle of Knowledge. All subjects wishing to enter the contest should appear at the Royal Palace of Tallysum tomorrow at noon."

Carrie's Mother: Can you believe this opportunity?

Carrie: I don't believe it! This is the chance of a lifetime! Oh, Mother, do you think I can possibly win?

Carrie's Mother: You are the smartest person I know. If anyone can win the prize, it is you!

Narrator 1: In the morning, Carrie dressed carefully in her best clothes. Just as the sun was coming up and the birds were beginning to sing, she set off on the long walk to the palace.

Narrator 2: She arrived at the palace exactly at noon and took her place in line. It did not help her nerves to see that she was the only girl in the room. She took a deep breath and tried to calm herself.

Narrator 1: One by one, the contestants stood before King Archibald. One by one, they failed to answer his questions correctly. Carrie's heart was pounding as she made her way to the front of the line.

King Archibald: Next!

Carrie: *(with a curtsey)* I'm next, Your Majesty.

King Archibald: *(laughing)* A girl, is it? All right, well I didn't say, "No girls allowed." Go ahead. See if you can answer my questions.

Carrie: Thank you, Your Majesty.

King Archibald: Question number one. You see before you a box. In the box there are black marbles and white marbles. If I were to blindfold you and ask you to pick a matching pair of marbles from the box, what is the smallest number of marbles you would have to pick out of the box to be CERTAIN that you had a matching pair? You have one minute to answer. Page, turn over the sand glass.

Page: *(snickering at Carrie)* Yes, sire. As you wish.

Carrie: *(to herself)* Well, if I picked two marbles, I might have two black ones or two white ones. In that case, I wouldn't need to pick another one. But I also might have one of each color. If that were the case, I would need to pick one more marble. This marble would be either black or white. It would therefore match at least one of the two marbles I had already chosen. In order to be CERTAIN, I would have to pick . . .

Carrie: *(shouts)* Three!

King Archibald: Well done, with time to spare. Are you ready for the next question?

Carrie: Yes, Your Majesty.

King Archibald: All right. You see before you a round spinner. I am going to flick the arrow with my finger and set the spinner in motion. Can you tell me, BEFORE I flick the arrow, what color the arrow will point to when it comes to rest? You have one minute to decide. Page, turn over the sand glass.

Page: *(quietly)* Yes, sire. As you wish.

Carrie: *(to herself)* Hmm, this is a more difficult question. There is no way to be sure of getting the right answer. But if I study the spinner, perhaps I can see what is most likely to happen. The spinner has 12 spaces on it. One space is red, one is green, and one is blue. The rest of the spaces are purple. That means that the arrow is most likely to land on purple. That has to be my answer.

Carrie: *(biting her lip and wringing her hands)* Purple! It should be purple!

Narrator 2: King Archibald flicked the arrow and it spun round and round. Carrie held her breath until the arrow finally came to rest on one of the purple spaces.

King Archibald: Well done, indeed! You have only one more question to answer and the scholarship is yours.

Carrie: Very well, Your Majesty.

King Archibald: You see before you two regular six-sided dice. When I roll the dice, the dots that show on their faces always add up to the numbers from 2 to 12. If I roll the dice 100 times, what number will come up most often? You have one minute. Page, turn over the sand glass.

Page: *(chuckling)* Yes, sire. As you wish. But she'll *never* get this one!

Carrie: Shhh! I'm thinking.

Carrie: *(to herself)* Another tricky question! Let me think . . . How many different ways are there to make each number? You can only roll a 2 by getting a 1 and a 1. How about a bigger number? You can get a 5 by rolling a 4 and a 1, or a 3 and a 2. You can get a 6 by rolling a 1 and a 5, a 2 and a 4, or a 3 and a 3. That's a lot of possibilities. Maybe that is the answer. But what about 7? Hmm, 1 and 6, 3 and 4, 5 and 2. The time is about to run out, oh dear . . .

Page: Ti—

Carrie: *(gasping)* Seven!

Page: Sire, the sand ran out!

King Archibald: She answered just in the nick of time, Page. Pipe down and hand me the dice. Let's see if she is right.

Narrator 1: King Archibald rolled the dice 100 times while the page kept a tally. Carrie jumped each time a seven showed on the dice. At the end, the king had rolled a two only 3 times. He had rolled a six 15 times. He had rolled an eight 11 times. But he had rolled a seven 19 times.

King Archibald: Congratulations, Carrie! You have won the scholarship! Can you begin your studies on Monday morning?

Carrie: *(joyfully)* Yes, oh yes! Thank you, Your Majesty.

Page: *(smiling in spite of himself)* Congratulations! I can't believe it! You really did it!

Carrie: Yes, I did. I am a very lucky girl.

Name _____

"Lucky" Predictions

At the end of the story, Carrie says she is a "very lucky girl." She knew how to solve the first problem accurately, but the next two problems required her to think about what was most likely to happen and then make a prediction.

Make a spinner and then try making some predictions of your own.

Materials:

paper fastener
paper clip

Put it together:

- First, color each spinner as indicated.
- Then list all of the possible outcomes of a spin for each spinner.
- Finally, record the most likely outcome.

1

red   red

red   red

red   black

Possible outcomes for Spinner 1:

Spinner lands on _____

Spinner lands on _____

The most likely outcome is _____

Possible outcomes for Spinner 2:

Spinner lands on _____

Spinner lands on _____

Spinner lands on _____

Spinner lands on _____

Spinner lands on _____

Spinner lands on _____

The most likely outcome is _____

For which spinner would it be easiest to predict the outcome? _____

Why? _____

_____

_____

2

blue   green

yellow   orange

yellow   orange

white   orange

white   purple

Lucky Seven

Is it true that 7 is the most frequently rolled number on a pair of dice?
Try it and see. Roll a pair of dice 100 times. Keep a tally of the numbers
that appear on the dice.

Dice Roll Tally Sheet

2	3	4	5	6	7	8	9	10	11	12
TOTAL	TOTAL	TOTAL	TOTAL	TOTAL	TOTAL	TOTAL	TOTAL	TOTAL	TOTAL	TOTAL

Which number (or numbers) appeared most frequently?

_____

Which number (or numbers) appeared least frequently?

_____

Now Presenting...

The Emperor's New Clothes

In this play based on the folktale by Hans Christian Andersen, an emperor and his subjects are all afraid to tell the truth for fear of appearing foolish. A young boy who is not afraid to be different speaks up and points out the truth.

11 parts

Setting the Stage

Background

Invite students to share their understanding of the term *peer pressure*. Be sure they understand that it is a pull to go along with the ideas or actions of a group in order to be part of that group and fit in. Ask students if they have ever felt pressure to say or do something in order to be like the rest of a group, even though it did not feel right. Remind students that peer pressure has many forms, and that even the wisest of adults can sometimes fall victim to the pressure to conform. Encourage students to talk about why it is so tempting to go along with the crowd, and why it can sometimes be difficult to do the right thing.

Staging

Arrange the staging area into four sections: palace court, weaving room, emperor's dressing room, and town lane.

Vocabulary

Introduce and discuss the following words before reading the script:

animatedly: excitedly

attribute: a quality; feature

compatriot: a fellow countryman

devise: to invent; create

fawn: to seek favor through false flattery or compliments

incompetent: lacking the qualities necessary to perform a particular job

swindle: to obtain money or goods through deceit or trickery

unique: very rare or uncommon; original

Now Presenting...

The Emperor's New Clothes

In this play based on the folktale by Hans Christian Andersen, an emperor and his subjects are all afraid to tell the truth for fear of appearing foolish. A young boy who is not afraid to be different speaks up and points out the truth.

Characters

Narrator 1 .... _____

Narrator 2 .... _____

Emperor .... _____

Emperor's Wife .... _____

Swindler 1 .... _____

Swindler 2 .... _____

Old Official .... _____

Young Official........................... _____

Villager 1 .... _____

Villager 2 .... _____

Young Boy .... _____

Readers' Theater, Grade 4 • EMC 3309

The Emperor's New Clothes

.... Characters ....

Narrator 1	Old Official
Narrator 2	Young Official
Emperor	Villager 1
Emperor's Wife	Villager 2
Swindler 1	Young Boy
Swindler 2	

Narrator 1: Many, many years ago there lived an emperor who loved new clothes. He spent all of his money on the latest hats, coats, gloves, jackets, trousers, and shoes. Of course, every article was made of the finest leather or the softest silk. Only the best materials would do! Even the hems on the emperor's robes were stitched with thread spun from gold.

Narrator 2: Every hour of every day, the emperor put on a new outfit. He couldn't bear for anyone—not even his loving wife—to see him dressed the same way twice. While other monarchs were busy with affairs of state, the emperor spent all his time riding about in his carriage, showing off each new suit of clothes. He sometimes went to the theater, but he was never interested in the play. He only wanted to be seen and admired for his spectacular fashion sense.

Narrator 2: An annual village festival was close at hand, and the emperor wanted a stunning new outfit.

Emperor: *(to his wife)* My dear, the procession along the town lane is next Saturday, and I don't have a thing to wear!

Emperor's Wife: Don't worry. I'm certain that the village tailor can design something you'd like.

Emperor: *(rolling his eyes)* Oh, please! The village tailor? He has already made hundreds of robes. Between you and me, I don't think he can come up with anything new. I want clothes that are really different, really stylish—something no one has seen before!

Narrator 1: It just so happened that two swindlers had come to the emperor's village. They had heard about the emperor's fascination with clothes, and had devised a way to cheat him out of a great deal of money.

Narrator 2: When they heard that the emperor wanted new clothes for the festival, the two swindlers wasted no time requesting an audience with the emperor and his wife.

Narrator 1: Posing as weavers, the swindlers strolled confidently into the palace.

Emperor: *(to the swindlers)* Welcome! We are honored to be in the presence of such famous world-class weavers. I understand you two are capable of creating the most exquisite cloth.

Swindler 1: *(pretending to be modest)* You are too kind, Your Majesty. My associate and I are simple weavers, though we do have, um, special skills.

Emperor's Wife: Special skills, eh? My husband requires a new suit of clothes for the upcoming festival. Would you be able to create something unique for him? Something truly spectacular?

Swindler 1: *(smiling)* Oh, most certainly, Your Majesty!

Narrator 2: The first swindler leaned over and whispered in the ear of his compatriot. He then turned and addressed the emperor.

Swindler 2: Your Highness, my partner and I can create a most exquisite robe for you. Not only are the colors and the patterns extraordinarily beautiful, but the material also has a rather remarkable attribute.

Emperor: *(intrigued)* Oh, do tell me! What is it?

Swindler 1: *(smiling)* This cloth is invisible to anyone who is incompetent or stupid.

Emperor: *(to his wife)* My dear, just imagine how valuable such cloth would be. If I had clothes made from such material, I would be able to see which of my officials is incompetent, and I would be able to tell the clever from the stupid!

Emperor's Wife: *(thinking)* Hmmm. It would be nice to know who in our court is smart and who is foolish . . .

Emperor: Then it is settled! *(to the swindlers)* I want you to begin immediately. I must have clothes made from your special cloth. Money is no object!

Narrator 2: And so the two swindlers set up their equipment in the weaving room and pretended to go to work, although there was nothing at all on the looms. They asked for the finest silk and the purest gold, all of which they hid away. The two worked for hours on the empty looms—often late into the night.

Narrator 1: With each passing minute, the emperor became more and more anxious.

Emperor: *(to himself)* I would really like to know how they are coming with the cloth. Of course, I shouldn't go down and bother them myself . . . Perhaps I'll send my honest old official. He will certainly be able to see the cloth: he is very clever, and he is quite competent in his position.

Narrator 2: So the emperor sent his honest official to the weaving room. When the old man entered the room, he saw the two swindlers working on an empty loom.

Old Official: *(to himself)* Goodness! I cannot see a thing!

Swindler 1: *(to Old Official)* Welcome, good sir! Tell us, how do you like the cloth?

Narrator 1: The swindlers pointed to the empty loom.

Swindler 2: Isn't it a beautiful design?

Swindler 1: Aren't the colors magnificent?

Old Official: *(to himself)* Is it possible that I am stupid? I have never thought so. Am I incompetent and unfit for my position? If anyone finds out, I'll be out of a job! No one must ever know this. No, it will never do for me to say that I was unable to see the material.

Swindler 2: Excuse me, sir? You aren't saying anything.

Old Official: *(raising his arms animatedly)* Oh, it is magnificent! It is the most exquisite of cloths! It is truly fabulous! Oh, my! The colors and the pattern are extraordinary! Yes, I will tell the emperor that I am very satisfied with it.

Narrator 2: The old official reported back to the emperor that the cloth was the finest imaginable. But the emperor was not satisfied. He sent another trusted official to see the cloth.

Narrator 1: The young official proceeded to the weaving room, where he saw the two swindlers working on an empty loom.

Young Official: *(to himself)* Oh no! The old official saw the cloth, and he said it was magnificent. But I can see nothing! Is it possible that I'm stupid? No one must know. I'll simply go along with what the old official said. That way, no one will find out that I'm incompetent.

Narrator 2: The young official told the emperor that the cloth was the most incredible that he had ever seen.

Young Official: *(to the emperor)* Your Majesty, the cloth is truly spectacular. You will be much admired by your subjects at the festival.

Narrator 1: The swindlers pretended to work day and night. They cut through the air with scissors, and they sewed with unthreaded needles. Finally, on the morning of the procession, they announced that they were done.

Narrator 2: The emperor and his wife welcomed the weavers to the royal dressing room.

Swindler 1: *(to the emperor)* Behold! The clothes are finished.

Narrator 1: The two swindlers raised their arms as though they were holding something.

Swindler 2: Your Highness, just look at these trousers. And here is the jacket and your robe!

Swindler 1: The cloth is as light as feathers. You might think you don't have a thing on, but that is one of the wonderful qualities of such fine cloth.

Emperor's Wife: *(to herself)* I cannot see a thing, but I mustn't let anyone know. I will simply go along with what the two officials said. *(to the Emperor)* My darling! It is truly unique! It is indeed perfect for you!

Emperor: *(to himself)* Oh no! My wife sees the cloth, but I cannot! I never thought I was stupid. No one must know. *(to his wife)* Yes! The cloth is amazing! I cannot wait to wear it in the procession!

Narrator 2: The emperor took off all his clothes, and the swindlers pretended to dress him, piece by piece. Then the emperor turned and looked into the mirror.

Swindler 2: *(fawning)* Oh, Your Highness! The clothes suit you so well. You look positively magnificent.

Narrator 1: With his wife on his arm, the emperor made his way down the town lane. Each person who saw him pretended to be amazed by the emperor's new clothes.

Villager 1: Look at that pattern on the robe! Isn't it wonderful?

Villager 2: Yes, but look at the colors on the jacket. How bold!

Narrator 2: Suddenly, a young boy's voice was heard as the procession passed by.

Young Boy: But he doesn't have anything on!

Narrator 1: A hush came over the crowd.

Villager 1: The boy's right. The emperor has no clothes!

Villager 2: It's true! The emperor has no clothes!

Narrator 2: And so an entire village was humbled by the sincerity of a child. Each person learned that it is better to be alone and honest, than to be with a crowd—and false.

 Readers' Theater, Grade 4 • EMC 3309

Name _____

What Would You Do?

Peer pressure is one of the themes of "The Emperor's New Clothes." Read each scenario below, and then write a response in which you stand up for what is right.

1. You are at a friend's house after school. She suggests calling the fire department to report a fire at an abandoned house down the block. She says it will be fun to see the fire engine racing down the street with its lights flashing and its sirens blaring. What do you do?

_____

_____

2. You are at the mall with several friends. You decide to purchase a CD at a crowded music store. You wait at the counter with the CD in hand, but you can't get anyone to help you. The CD does not have an electronic tag, and your friends say you should just pocket it and leave. After all, the store obviously doesn't want your business, otherwise a sales associate would have rung you up by now. What do you do?

_____

_____

3. You are taking an end-of-grade test at school. You know you must pass this test to move to the next grade. Your best friend asks you to share your answers during the exam. You don't want to let your friend down, yet you don't want to put your final grades at risk. What do you do?

_____

_____

4. You go to the movies with several friends. All through the movie, you're bored beyond belief. Afterwards, each of your friends goes on and on about how terrific the movie was. They then turn to you and ask what you thought. You're tempted to say you liked it too. What do you do?

_____

_____

Name _____

One Story, Many Cultures

"The Emperor's New Clothes" is a Danish folktale by Hans Christian Andersen. Did you know that there are similar stories told in places all around the world? In Sri Lanka they call this tale "The Invisible Silk Robe." Storytellers in Turkey relate the story of "The King's New Turban."

Use the outline below to plan your own story about being truthful, despite pressure to do otherwise. Then use the completed outline to write your own tale. Share it with your classmates or family.

Title _____

This story is about _____

_____

This story takes place _____

_____

The action begins when _____

_____

Then _____

_____

Next, _____

_____

After that, _____

_____

The story ends when _____

_____

_____

Readers' Theater, Grade 4 • EMC 3309

Now Presenting...

Sarah's Gold

A young woman seeks her fortune during the California gold rush.

Setting the Stage

Background

Be sure your students are familiar with the history of the Gold Rush that began in 1849, when gold was discovered in California. Prospectors rushed from all corners of the world to stake a claim and search for gold. They came by covered wagon, on foot, and by sea. Crude towns and tent villages sprang up all over California as gold seekers by the tens of thousands poured into the area. While most of them were men, women also have a place in the history of the Gold Rush.

Explain to students that Sarah (the main character in this play) is a fictional character, but her story is based on real events that happened to real women. Help students understand these reasons that Sarah might have had for going to California by ship:

- She lived in Boston, a large seaport where travel by ship was common and convenient.

- A sea voyage, though long and dangerous, was more acceptable and familiar than overland travel.

- It would have been extremely difficult for a single woman to join a wagon train unless accompanied by her family.

Staging

Clear two areas: one on the east side of the classroom and the other on the west. Explain that Boston is on the eastern coast of the United States and that San Francisco is on the western coast. Set the beginning scenes of the script in the area to the east. Have Sarah move across the classroom and perform the rest of the script in the area to the west.

Vocabulary

Introduce and discuss the following words before reading the script:

bustle: noisy, energetic activity

folly: lacking good sense; foolishness

gallivant: to travel or wander about for pleasure

harbor: a part of a body of water deep enough for ships to anchor there

meager: scant; lacking fullness or richness

nugget: a solid lump, especially of a precious metal

pouch: a small bag closed with a drawstring

prospector: someone who explores an area in search of minerals

scandal: a disgrace

vouch: to verify or support

Now Presenting...

Sarah's Gold

A young woman seeks her fortune during the California gold rush.

Characters

Narrator 1 .... ———————————————

Narrator 2 .... ———————————————

Sarah .... ———————————————

Kate.. ———————————————

Miss Finley .... ———————————————

Prospector Joe............................. ———————————————

Prospector Mike .... ———————————————

Prospector John.......................... ———————————————

Banker Bates .... ———————————————

Readers' Theater, Grade 4 • EMC 3309

Sarah's Gold

························· **Characters** ·························

Narrator 1   Prospector Joe
Narrator 2   Prospector Mike
Sarah   Prospector John
Kate   Banker Bates
Miss Finley

Narrator 1: In the summer of 1849, the streets of Boston buzzed with conversation about California.

Narrator 2: Gold had been discovered in California. Young men were packing their belongings and boarding ships bound for the goldfields, sure that they would make their fortunes.

Narrator 1: Sarah Kirby was an 18-year-old schoolteacher who lived in Boston. She too longed to go to California to seek her fortune.

Narrator 2: One hot afternoon, Sarah and her sister Kate were walking down beside the harbor. They stood and watched as a ship bound for San Francisco sailed out to sea.

Sarah: Oh, Kate, I want to go to California! I would go tomorrow if I could find a captain willing to take me on his ship.

Kate: You can't be serious! A young, single woman like you can't be gallivanting off to California! What a scandal!

Sarah: I don't care about scandal. I want to go and seek my fortune. In fact, I am going to do it. I have been saving my money for a long time.

Kate: You will never find a captain who will accept a female passenger. Sarah, you must forget about this crazy dream of yours!

Narrator 1: But Sarah could not forget. She wrote letters to all the shipping firms asking if she could buy a ticket on one of their ships. Always the answer was the same: a firm "no."

Narrator 2: The ships were full of rough and sometimes dangerous men. The voyage was long and difficult, and the captains did not want to have to worry about the safety of a young woman traveling alone.

Narrator 1: But Sarah was a very determined young woman, and she kept writing letters. At last came the answer she had been hoping for.

Sarah: Kate, look! A letter from Baxter and Howe Shipping!

Kate: The answer will be the same, Sarah. Why can't you forget this folly?

Sarah: *(reading the letter to Kate, with excitement)* Dear Miss Kirby, I am pleased to inform you that our shipping firm would be most happy to offer you passage to San Francisco. Our ship, the *El Dorado,* is departing from Boston next week on the 18th of October 1849. Several ladies will be on board. We have arranged for a separate cabin and...

Sarah: *(dancing around the room)* I'm going to California, Kate! I'm going! I'm really going!

Narrator 2: Sarah packed her clothes and books into a trunk and bid a tearful farewell to her family. But as soon as the ship was underway, her tears were forgotten. She was bound for California! Her dream was coming true.

Narrator 1: It took eight long months to make the voyage around the tip of South America, but at last the *El Dorado* dropped its anchor in San Francisco's beautiful blue bay. Sarah set out into the city to find a job.

Narrator 2: She went first to a boarding school that some Boston friends had told her about. The school was in a large house on Market Street. Sarah knocked, and a serious but kindly woman opened the door.

Miss Finley: May I help you?

Sarah: Yes, ma'am. My name is Sarah Kirby. I have come to inquire whether you need a teacher at your school. I am well qualified. I have some letters that vouch for my character.

Miss Finley: Actually, I do need some help. I can offer you a position as my assistant. The pay will be $45 per month. You will teach the youngest children during the day. In the evening you will help with the baking.

Sarah: Oh, thank you, Miss Finley. I am so happy to be here.

Narrator 1: Sarah cheerfully went to work. She loved everything about California. The town bustled with life and noise. Prospectors filled the streets at all hours of the day and night. To Sarah, it was all wonderful and exciting.

Narrator 2: However, Sarah found it difficult to survive on her meager pay. One evening as she was placing a cherry pie on the windowsill to cool, a prospector happened by.

Prospector Joe: Miss, I'll give you $5 in gold for that handsome pie.

Sarah: Excuse me, sir. What did you say?

Prospector Joe: I said, Miss, I'll give you $5 for that pie.

Narrator 1: Sarah stared at the man, thinking that her ears were playing tricks on her.

Prospector: If you don't want to sell it for $5, I'll give you $10. Here.

Narrator 2: He thrust a small pouch full of gold dust and nuggets into Sarah's hand, picked up the hot pie, and walked away whistling.

Sarah: *(to herself)* Whoever heard of such a thing! A simple pie for $10!

Narrator 1: The next day, Sarah told Miss Finley that she was leaving her job. She went to the store and bought flour, sugar, and other supplies. She bought a tent and an iron skillet. She found a place in a nearby gold camp to pitch her tent, and she began to bake pies.

Narrator 2: Sarah baked pies by the hundreds. As the weeks and months passed, word of Sarah's mouth-watering pies traveled from camp to camp. No matter how many she made, there were hungry miners lined up outside her tent waiting to buy more.

Prospector Mike: Miss Sarah, these here are the best pies in the world.

Sarah: Thank you, Mike. I am glad you boys like them so much.

Prospector John: Yep, I get powerful mad when I get in from the diggin's and find Miss Sarah sold out of pies. 'Specially apple. That's my favorite.

Sarah: If I had a cookstove I could bake more pies, and I would never run out. You could all have your favorites every day.

Prospector John: Mr. Wright over at the dry goods store just got in a fresh shipment of stuff from back east. I saw two cookstoves being hoisted off the ship.

Sarah: Oh, John, is that really true? I have plenty of money saved. I'll buy the stove if you boys will find a wagon and carry it over here for me.

Narrator 1: The prospectors were happy to help. They delivered the cookstove and set it up in the little cabin that had taken the place of Sarah's tent.

Narrator 2: The cabin had a dirt floor, but it had a strong roof that kept out the rain. And now it had a real stove. Sarah was overjoyed. She made more pies and more money than ever before. Weeks passed.

Narrator 1: One morning, Sarah woke early and decided to clean the cabin before she began her baking.

Narrator 2: She grabbed the willow broom from the corner and began to sweep the packed earth of the cabin floor. Suddenly, she noticed a gleam of yellow in the early morning light. Grabbing a spoon, she pried a gold nugget as big as the end of her thumb out of her cabin floor.

Sarah: *(to herself)* My heavens! My stars! Oh for Pete's sake!

Narrator 1: Sarah threw aside her broom and ran for a shovel. She tossed her few bits of furniture out of the cabin and began to dig. She forgot all about making pies.

Prospector Mike and Prospector John: Miss Sarah, have you got any pies?

Sarah: Sorry, Mike. Sorry, John. No pies today.

Narrator 2: Sarah dug in her cabin floor all that day, and the next and the next. After three days digging, she had a pail nearly full of sizable nuggets, which she took to the bank.

Banker Bates: Miss Kirby, I have weighed your nuggets. You have over two thousand dollars worth of gold here! Added to the money you have already deposited in this bank, you are quite a wealthy young lady.

Sarah: Yes, sir, I suppose I am. And I'm just getting started!

Banker Bates: But you don't need to work so hard, Miss Kirby. You could find a nice young man and settle down, get married.

Sarah: Maybe someday, Banker Bates, maybe someday. For the moment, I find that this hard work agrees with me. I like living my own life and making my own money. I'm going to build a small house with a very large kitchen and two of the biggest cookstoves you have ever seen. I'm going to hire some women to help me with the baking. I'll soon be back with *two* buckets full of gold!

Narrator 1: And that is exactly what she did.

Name _____

Pay Dirt!

Sarah was very excited when she found the gold nugget in the dirt floor of her cabin. Think of a time when you found something unexpected. What did you find? How did you feel? Write a paragraph about the experience. Then draw a picture to illustrate it.

_____

_____

_____

_____

_____

Name _____

Seek Your Fortune

Many people in the gold camps made a lot of money. Some of them were miners who found lots of gold. Others were people who provided services for the gold miners. These people—many of whom were women—ran boarding houses, restaurants, bakeries, and laundries.

If you were suddenly transported to a gold camp in California during the 1850s, would you try to find gold or would you offer a service to the gold miners? Which do you think would be the best way to make a fortune? Give at least three reasons to support your answer.

Now Presenting...

The Boy Who Drew Cats

This classic Japanese folktale tells the story of a young boy who stays true to himself—and is rewarded.

13 parts

Setting the Stage

Background

Share with students these words, written by the famous English playwright William Shakespeare: "To thine own self be true." Brainstorm about the meaning of this phrase. Have students explain, using examples from their own lives, why it is important to be true to oneself. Tell students that this script is about a young boy whose natural talents are a mystery to those around him—until they prove very useful one night.

Staging

Arrange the staging area in three sections: the farm, the country temple, and the city temple.

Vocabulary

Introduce and discuss the following words before reading the script:

defile: to make filthy; to make a sacred space unclean

elder: an older or aged person

flee: to run away; escape

halfhearted: lacking interest or feeling

keen: enthusiastic; sharp-witted

The Boy Who Drew Cats

This classic Japanese folktale tells the story of a young boy who stays true to himself—and is rewarded.

Characters

Narrator 1 .... _____

Narrator 2 .... _____

Farmer .... _____

Farmer's Wife .... _____

Boy .... _____

Boy's Older Brother .... _____

Boy's Sister 1 .... _____

Boy's Sister 2 .... _____

Country Temple Priest .... _____

Rat Goblin .... _____

Villager 1 .... _____

Villager 2 .... _____

City Temple Priest .... _____

The Boy Who Drew Cats

·············· **Characters** ··············

Narrator 1   Boy's Sister 2
Narrator 2   Country Temple Priest
Farmer   Rat Goblin
Farmer's Wife   Villager 1
Boy   Villager 2
Boy's Older Brother   City Temple Priest
Boy's Sister 1

Narrator 1: Once upon a time, in a small Japanese village, there lived a poor farmer and his wife.

Narrator 2: The farmer and his wife had two sons and two daughters. The two daughters were very strong, and they helped their mother in the house and garden.

Narrator 1: The elder son was also very strong, and he helped his father in the rice fields. But the younger son was small and frail. He was very clever, but he was not strong enough to help his father plant or harvest the rice.

Farmer's Wife: *(to the farmer)* Husband, I am very lucky to have such strong daughters. They are a blessing to us indeed!

Boy's Sister 1: *(smiling)* Mother, I enjoy helping you in the garden. I love to plant the seeds, to weed the rows, and to see the vegetables grow.

Boy's Sister 2: *(smiling)* Mother, I enjoy helping you in the house. I like to see the shine of the newly polished floor, and I take pleasure in the crispness of newly ironed sheets.

Farmer: *(to his wife)* Wife, we are indeed blessed to have such fine daughters! I know they are certainly a comfort to you. And we are also blessed with a strong and helpful elder son. Every day he helps me in the rice fields. As I grow older, I find the planting and harvesting increasingly difficult. It gladdens my heart to see him take pleasure in the workings of the farm.

Boy's Older Brother: Father, I do enjoy the work in the fields. I love the feel of the sun on my back, and I love the breeze in my face. And there is nothing more pleasant than the smell of the air right before it rains.

Farmer: *(to his wife)* But what are we to do about our younger son? He is too small to be of any use on the farm. He does his best when I ask him to help his brother and me. But he cannot do the simplest of tasks. If I ask him to carry the pail, he drops it!

Farmer's Wife: I know, I know. I have asked him to help his sisters and me around the house, but he seems incapable of even the easiest chores. He burns the sheets when he irons them, and he undercooks the fish!

Farmer: Wife, our son is frail and small, but he is very clever. Perhaps the old priest at the country temple will take him as an apprentice.

Farmer's Wife: What a good idea, husband! I'm sure our bright and imaginative younger son will impress the old priest.

Narrator 2: The next day the farmer took his son to the country temple. The old priest asked the boy many difficult questions, but the boy answered them well. After all, he had a keen mind and a clever imagination.

Country Temple Priest: Boy, what is the color of the sky?

Boy: When it is summer, the sky is a bright blue with fluffy patches of white. When it is winter, the sky is a dark and heavy gray. When it is morning, the sky is many glorious shades of pink. When it is evening, the sky is the darkest of reds.

Country Temple Priest: *(stroking his chin)* Hmmm. Boy, what is the sound of one hand clapping?

Boy: It is the sound of halfhearted gladness. True joy is expressed with the clapping of both hands.

Country Temple Priest: *(to the farmer)* Your son is quite clever. I will take him as an apprentice.

 Readers' Theater, Grade 4 • EMC 3309

Narrator 1: The farmer returned home, and the boy stayed at the country temple. He was a good apprentice, and he obeyed the priest, but he had one failing. Instead of studying his lessons, the boy drew cats instead. He could not help himself. In his heart, the boy was an artist.

Narrator 2: The boy drew all kinds of cats. He drew orange cats and yellow cats, striped cats and spotted cats. He drew big cats, small cats, wild cats, and tame cats. He drew cats all over his books and all over the floors. He even drew cats on the fine rice paper screens in the temple!

Country Temple Priest: Boy, why do you draw these cats? You know you should be studying.

Boy: I'm sorry, sir. I know I should be working on my lessons, but I cannot help myself. You see, I am truly an artist in my heart.

Country Temple Priest: I am saddened by your inability to obey me. I like you very much, but I'm afraid I must send you back to your family. Pack your things and return home. But remember this one important piece of advice: Avoid large places at night; keep to small.

Narrator 1: The boy did not know what the old priest meant, but he packed his belongings and left the temple.

Boy: *(to himself)* If I go back to the farm, my father will punish me. I will go to the city instead, and see if any of the priests in the temple there need an apprentice.

Narrator 2: It was dark when the boy arrived at the city gates. He made his way to the temple, and he knocked on the door. No one answered. He knocked again, but still no one answered.

Boy: *(to himself)* This is very odd. Perhaps the door is unlocked.

Narrator 1: The boy pushed on the door, and it opened. He called out for the priest, but no one answered. What the boy didn't know was that a huge rat goblin had taken over the temple! The priests had all fled. Soldiers had been called in, but not even they could drive out the rat goblin.

Boy: *(to himself)* There is a room in the corner. I will go there and wait for the priests to return.

Narrator 2: The boy went into the room to wait. He pulled out some rice paper, pens, and ink from his bag and began to draw cats. The boy drew big cats, small cats, thin cats, and tall cats. He drew happy cats and ferocious cats. He drew fat cats and skinny cats.

Narrator 1: When the boy filled up his paper, he drew cats on the floor. When he filled up the floor, he drew cats on the walls. Finally, when he had covered the room with pictures of cats, the boy became tired.

Boy: *(to himself)* I am very sleepy. But I remember what the old priest in the country temple told me: Avoid large places at night; keep to small. There is a small cupboard along the wall. I will crawl in the cupboard and sleep. Perhaps tomorrow the priests will return.

Narrator 2: The boy quickly fell asleep. But it wasn't long before he was awakened by a horrible sound.

Rat Goblin: *(growling)* Who is here? Who is in my temple? I smell a young boy! Who is defiling my home?

Narrator 1: Just then the boy heard more strange sounds.

Rat Goblin: *(surprised)* What's this? What's this? Arrghhh!

Boy: *(to himself)* What is going on? It sounds like fighting! I hear yelps and screams and howls and growls! I hear bumping and thumping and crashing and thrashing!

Narrator 2: The boy peaked out from the cupboard, but he couldn't see anything through the darkness. He decided it was safest to stay where he was until morning.

Narrator 1: At dawn the boy crept from his hiding place, and what did he see? The enormous rat goblin, dead on the floor!

Boy: *(to himself)* A goblin! No wonder the temple was empty! But who could have killed such a thing?

Narrator 2: Just then the boy noticed something strange about the cats in the pictures he had drawn all around the room. The fur around each cat's mouth was red with blood!

Boy: *(to himself)* How can this be? The cats have killed the goblin!

Narrator 1: When the priests of the temple and the people of the village learned that the rat goblin had been defeated, they declared the boy a hero.

Villager 1: You have saved our village from the goblin!

Villager 2: Even the mightiest of our soldiers could not defeat the goblin. But you, a small and frail boy, have saved us! Tell us, how did you survive?

Boy: I simply remembered what the old priest at the country temple told me: Avoid large places at night; keep to small.

City Temple Priest: Ah, you are a very clever boy. I would be honored to have you as an apprentice. You may stay here at the temple as long as you like.

Boy: Thank you, sir. But I no longer wish to apprentice as a priest. I am an artist in my heart, and an artist I must be.

Narrator 2: The boy left the village, and it was not long before he became a famous artist. His pictures of cats were known throughout Japan. And from town to town, people told the story of how a goblin had been defeated by a small boy who drew cats.

Origami Cat

Origami is the traditional Japanese art of folding paper. Follow these directions to make an origami cat.

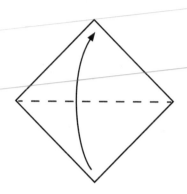

1) Fold in half

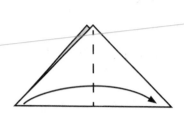

2) Fold in half again

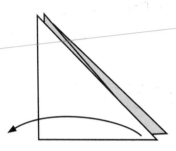

3) Open up

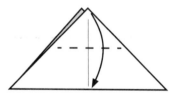

4) Fold top to bottom

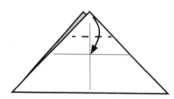

5) Fold top to center point

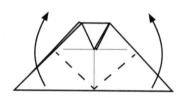

6) Fold tips up

7) Fold bottom tip up

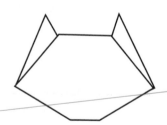

8) Flip over

9) Add facial features

Name _____

Haiku

Haiku is a traditional form of Japanese poetry that is over 600 years old.
Haiku is made up of unrhymed verse in three lines:

- The first line has five syllables.
- The second line has seven syllables.
- The last line has five syllables.

Haiku tries to capture an image in just three lines. Here is a sample haiku based
on "The Boy Who Drew Cats":

An artist at heart
The boy struggles to be true
To his own nature

Try writing your own haikus based on the story.

_____

_____

_____

_____

_____

_____

Now Presenting...

The Story of the Chestnut Tree

The story of the chestnut tree is one of an environmental disaster—although a happy ending may still be possible.

Setting the Stage

Background

You and your students may not know that 100 years ago, the chestnut tree was the king of the American forest. Tell students that chestnut trees grew to over 100 feet in height. In the Appalachian Mountains, one of every four hardwood trees was an American chestnut.

But in 1904 a blight struck chestnut trees in New York. It quickly spread throughout the country. In just a few years, almost all the chestnut trees were dead or dying. This blight has been called one of the worst environmental disasters in U.S. history.

Fortunately, many seeds from these trees were saved, and scientists are working to breed a new American chestnut tree that will be resistant to the blight. Perhaps one day these leafy giants will once again stand proudly in our forests.

Vocabulary

Introduce and discuss the following words before reading the script:

blight: a disease causing the injury or death of a plant

damage: harm or injury

fungus: a type of plant that can live on or in another living thing

organism: an animal, plant, bacterium, or other living thing made up of various systems that work together

resist: to be able to withstand or fight back

sprout: to begin to grow

whittle: to shape an object by cutting thin shavings from wood with a knife

Now Presenting...

The Story of the Chestnut Tree

The story of the chestnut tree is one of an environmental disaster—although a happy ending may still be possible.

Characters

Narrator .... ———————————————

Sam.. ———————————————

Jake .... ———————————————

Maria .... ———————————————

Dad .... ———————————————

Grandpa .... ———————————————

Mr. Weaver .... ———————————————

Mrs. Weaver............................... ———————————————

Readers' Theater, Grade 4 • EMC 3309

The Story of the Chestnut Tree

······················ **Characters** ······················

Narrator   Dad
Sam   Grandpa
Jake   Mr. Weaver
Maria   Mrs. Weaver

Narrator: The Boykin children—Sam, Jake, and Maria—spend almost every Saturday with their grandpa. Today, when the children and their father arrive at Grandpa's house, they find him in his workshop. He is whittling on a chunk of wood.

Sam: Hi Grandpa. What're you doing?

Grandpa: I'm carving something. Come take a look.

Jake: It's a bear!

Sam: Wow, that's awesome.

Maria: It almost looks real!

Dad: That is pretty cool, Pop. The wood is really interesting. It's kind of red. What is it?

Grandpa: Oh, this is interesting wood, all right. It has a history. In fact, it used to be part of my own grandpa's old barn. But that isn't the most special thing about this wood. No, the most special thing about this wood is that it came from a chestnut tree.

Narrator: The children looked at each other, and then at Dad. But he just shrugged his shoulders.

Dad: What is so special about that?

Grandpa: Don't you know the story of the chestnut tree?

Dad, Jake, Sam, and Maria: No!

Grandpa: Well, the story of the chestnut tree is one of a big disaster! It's a terrible story. Are you sure you want to hear it?

Dad, Jake, Sam, and Maria: Yes!

Grandpa: All right. Here goes. Way back when, when I was just a boy, there were chestnut trees all through these hills. Most of them were dead or dying, mind you, but they were still here. We'd go out and gather up chestnuts by the sackful. Man, they were good eating. You had to wear gloves, though, 'cause every single nut had a sharp, spiny case around it.

Sam: Was it really worth the trouble?

Grandpa: You bet it was. Those nuts were de-licious.

Jake: Go on, Grandpa, tell the story.

Grandpa: Back when my dad was a boy, the chestnut trees were everywhere. They were big, healthy trees then. They'd stand a hundred feet tall or more, and their branches spread out big and shady. My dad told me once that there were so many chestnut trees that a squirrel could've made a run from Maine to Virginia without ever touching the ground! Mind you, I can't say if that's true, but I know there were lots and lots of chestnut trees.

Maria: What happened to them, Grandpa?

Grandpa: They got sick.

Sam: What do you mean, they got sick? How can a tree get sick?

Grandpa: Trees get sick about like we do, kids. Tiny little organisms get inside and cause damage. In this case, it's called a blight.

Jake: Couldn't they just get some kind of medicine? That's what we do when we get sick.

Grandpa: Nobody knew how to stop the blight. They tried all kinds of things, of course, but none of them worked. The blight kept spreading from tree to tree. As time passed, more and more of the trees died away. It really was sad.

Maria: Weren't there lots of other kinds of trees? Why did it matter if the chestnut trees died?

Grandpa: Well, it mattered for quite a few reasons. First off, the chestnut was the most important tree in the forest. About a fourth of all the trees in these mountains were chestnuts, so when they died they left an awful gap.

Dad: That must have been hard on lots of animals.

Sam: Why would the animals care?

Grandpa: They'd care because the chestnut tree was their grocery store! Birds and squirrels, bears and deer, all kinds of animals relied on the good old chestnut for food. It was full of protein and fat and all the nutrients the animals needed.

Jake: I bet some animals lived in the chestnut trees too!

Grandpa: You'd win that bet, Jake. Why those big old trees were regular apartment buildings for birds and squirrels and such. Of course, a lot of people were also pretty upset about losing the chestnut trees.

Maria: They wanted chestnuts to eat, didn't they?

Grandpa: That's right. People *did* miss the chestnuts. But that's not all, not by a long shot.

Dad: Did the trees make good lumber?

Grandpa: The best! You see, chestnut wood was light but strong. The trees grew straight and tall and the trunks were big around. Some say they could fill a whole boxcar with the lumber cut from a single tree! And it made the greatest fence posts ever.

Sam: Why were the fence posts so good?

Grandpa: When you put a fence post in the ground, the moisture in the earth seeps in and the wood starts to rot away. But not chestnut wood. Something in the wood keeps it from rotting. In the old days, everybody used chestnut for fence posts. *(sigh)* Not anymore.

Dad: Did every single chestnut tree die? Didn't any of them survive?

Grandpa: All the trees died. Every one. But squirrels had stashed plenty of chestnuts away in the woods. So the trees kept coming up. Even today, they sprout up here and there. But the fungus that causes the blight is still around. It's in the soil. And when a new tree sprouts, it grows along okay for awhile, then it gets sick and dies.

Jake: Isn't there anything we can do about it?

Grandpa: Folks are trying, Jake. You remember Mr. Weaver who lives up the road? He has a little stand of young chestnut trees on his farm.

Dad: Why is he growing chestnuts if they're just going to die?

Grandpa: Let's go see him, and you can ask him! I think you'll be intrigued.

Narrator: The family piled into the car and drove a short distance on the highway before turning into a bumpy gravel driveway. They pulled up in front of a neat white house where a man and a woman—both in overalls—greeted them.

Mr. Weaver: Hi folks!

Mrs. Weaver: How nice to see you!

Grandpa: These curious young ones want to see a real live chestnut tree! Can you help us out?

Mr. Weaver: Why sure. In fact, you're standing right next to one.

Mrs. Weaver: Yes, this is the oldest tree we have. It's going on seven years old. See where the bark is peeling away? That's from the blight. But we got a good crop of nuts from it this year.

Jake: Did you eat them?

Mr. Weaver: No, we sent them to a lab in Charlottesville. They're raising lots of chestnut trees and trying to solve this problem. They are crossing our chestnuts with Asian chestnut trees. You see, Asian chestnuts don't get sick with blight.

Sam: Well, why don't we just grow Asian chestnut trees then?

Mrs. Weaver: Asian chestnuts are much smaller trees. The chestnuts and lumber they produce just aren't as good. But they can resist the blight. Scientists are trying to figure out a way to blend the two kinds of trees together.

Grandpa: They hope to create a new tree that is big and beautiful and useful like the American chestnut, but able to resist blight like the Asian chestnut.

Mr. Weaver: I'm very hopeful. Perhaps one day chestnut trees will once again stand proudly in the forest.

Maria: That would give the story of the chestnut tree a very happy ending!

Chestnut Facts

A **fact** tells information that is true. An **opinion** gives someone's thoughts or feelings. Decide whether each sentence states a fact or gives an opinion.

1. Chestnuts have sharp, spiny coverings.	fact	opinion
2. Chestnuts taste good.	fact	opinion
3. Animals like to eat chestnuts.	fact	opinion
4. It is sad that the chestnut trees died.	fact	opinion
5. It is very important to save these trees.	fact	opinion

Write one additional fact about the American chestnut tree.

_____

_____

_____

_____

Write your own opinion about the American chestnut tree.

_____

_____

_____

_____

Name _____

Synonyms Are Similar

A **synonym** is a word that means the same thing, or about the same thing, as another word. Match each word with its synonym.

live	bumpy
sharp	damage
carve	blight
withstand	spiny
harm	resist
disease	survive
boards	whittle
rough	lumber

Answer these questions using complete sentences.

1. What is something you might build out of lumber? _____

_____

2. What kind of tool would you need in order to whittle? _____

_____

3. What object has a bumpy surface? _____

_____

4. What is something that a baby could damage? _____

_____

Answer Key

Louis Pasteur: A Scientist Serving Humanity

page 15: Answers will vary. Make sure students use standard letter-writing conventions and mention something that Joseph Meister is grateful for in Letter 1 and something Louis Pasteur is grateful for in Letter 2.

page 16: Pasteur, research, germs, shots, France, Louis, bacteria, science, immunize, disease, laboratory, rabies, microbe, vaccine; pasteurization

The Girls of the Round Table

page 24: Students' emblems will vary, but each should include at least three symbols.

page 25: Responses will vary, but should include 5 to 10 appropriate activities in each column.

The Farmer, His Son, and Their Donkey

page 32: Across: 4) fast; 7) harsh; 11) agreeable; 12) bewildered; **Down:** 1) lash; 2) prance; 3) ashamed; 5) trudge; 6) moral; 8) dolt; 9) jeer; 10) clod

page 33: Answers will vary.

Keelboat Annie

page 42: Students' pictures should show Annie with dark skin and wild hair (page 39, paragraph 5), tall (page 39, paragraph 3), with a necklace of teeth wrapped around her neck (page 40, paragraph 11). She could be pulling a keelboat (page 39, paragraph 1), carrying barrels of cotton (page 39, paragraph 5), fighting with bullies (page 39, paragraph 7), or sitting on a seesaw with a bull (page 39, paragraph 3).

page 43: 1) sample; 2) T; 3) E—The Mississippi River has many tributaries.; 4) T; 5) E—Miss Annie was a tall, strong woman.; 6) E—Miss Annie liked to ride seesaws. OR Miss Annie liked to have fun.; 7) T; 8) T; 9) E—Miss Annie did not like bullies.

An Underwater Web of Life

pages 50 and 51: Be sure that the food web follows this order: sea and sun; diatoms; zooplankton; krill; herring; squid; codfish; seal; orca. Individual retellings will vary, but should follow this sequence.

page 52: Orca: mammal, warmblooded, have live babies. **Codfish:** fish, coldblooded, lay eggs. **Both:** live in the sea, breathe oxygen, good swimmers, predators.

How Coyote Brought Fire to the People: A Native American Legend

page 60: Answers will vary, but should demonstrate logical thinking and be supported with sound rationales. Uses of fire include heat, cooking, and light. Students may think of additional uses.

page 61: Answers will vary, but should include fictional as well as factual information about animals.
Coyote—Fiction: Coyote stole fire for people. **Fact:** Coyotes are scavengers.
Squirrel—Fiction: The fire hurt Squirrel's back so badly that her tail curled up.; Squirrel ran with the fire. **Fact:** Squirrels have bushy, curled tails.; Squirrels run swiftly.
Chipmunk—Fiction: The Fire Beings scratched Chipmunk's back. **Fact:** Chipmunks have white stripes on their backs.
Frog—Fiction: The Fire Beings pulled off frog's tail. **Fact:** Frogs don't have tails.

The Sager Children

page 69: Answers will vary.

page 70: 1) forlorn; 2) hopeful; 3) grateful; 4) brave; 5) joyful; 6) anxious; 7) concerned; 8) heartbroken; overjoyed

The Timekeepers

page 78: 1) **Egyptian sun clock—Advantages:** easy to make; portable. **Disadvantages—**doesn't work in the dark or on cloudy days; someone has to turn it around at noon
2) **Chinese water clock—Advantages:** small enough to be portable. **Disadvantages—**must have water available; only keeps time for one or a few hours
3) **Hourglass—Advantages:** easy to use. **Disadvantages—**someone has to turn it if you want to keep time for longer periods

page 79: 1) 7:20 a.m.; 2) 3:30 p.m.; 3) 35 minutes late; 4) 4:50 p.m.

Sojourner Truth: A Life Devoted to Justice

page 87: 1) F—Isabella's father was named Baumfree because he was tall and stood straight like a tree.; 2) F—Isabella was sold away from her family when she was 9 years old.; 3) T; 4) T; 5) F—Isabella ran away from Mr. Dumont in the light of day.; 6) T; 7) T; 8) F—In 1851 Sojourner Truth attended the Women's Rights Convention in Akron, Ohio.; 9) F—Frances Gage did allow Sojourner Truth to speak at the Convention.; 10) T

page 88: Designs will vary, but should include an acknowledgment of some of Truth's accomplishments.

How Animals Got Their Beautiful Coats

page 96: Paragraphs will vary, but be sure that students compare and/or contrast at least three attributes of each animal.

page 97: Answers will vary, but may include the following lessons: kindness is rewarded with kindness; people always show their true "colors"; people often get what they deserve, etc.

The Chance of a Lifetime

page 105: Possible outcomes for spinner 1: spinner lands on red; spinner lands on black; The most likely outcome is red.

Possible outcomes for spinner 2: spinner lands on yellow; spinner lands on blue; spinner lands on orange; spinner lands on white; spinner lands on purple; spinner lands on green; The most likely outcome is orange.

It would be easiest to predict the outcome of spinner 1 because it has the greatest area of a single color. Therefore, the spinner will most often land on that color.

page 106: Answers will vary. It may be interesting to tally class results on a chart.

The Emperor's New Clothes

page 114: Students' responses will vary. Consider using responses as springboards for class discussion about peer pressure.

page 115: Stories will vary, but make sure they relate to the stated theme.

Sarah's Gold

page 123: Answers will vary.

page 124: Answers will vary. Make sure each answer is supported by three reasons.
Possible reasons to support gold mining—It is more adventurous.; One big strike would make you rich.; It would be nice to work outdoors.
Possible reasons to support offering a service—The income is more dependable.; The work is not quite as hard.; You could work indoors.

The Boy Who Drew Cats

page 133: Poems will vary, but ascertain that they are in the correct format: three lines with five, seven, and five syllables, respectively.

The Story of the Chestnut Tree

page 141: 1) fact; 2) opinion; 3) fact; 4) opinion; 5) fact; Examples of additional facts and opinions about the American chestnut tree will vary.

page 142:

Answers will vary, but should make sense. Possibilities include: 1) You might build a house out of lumber.; 2) You need a knife and wood in order to whittle.; 3) A golf ball has a bumpy surface.; 4) A baby could damage a book.